How Civil Institutions Build Resilie~

Organizational Practices Derived from A Literature and Case Studies

Krista S. Langeland, David Manheim, Gary McLeod, George Nacouzi

RAND Project AIR FORCE

Prepared for the United States Air Force
Approved for public release; distribution unlimited

For more information on this publication, visit www.rand.org/t/RR1246

Library of Congress Cataloging-in-Publication Data is available for this publication.

ISBN: 978-0-8330-9201-4

Published by the RAND Corporation, Santa Monica, Calif.

© Copyright 2016 RAND Corporation

RAND® is a registered trademark.

Support RAND
Make a tax-deductible charitable contribution at
www.rand.org/giving/contribute

www.rand.org

Preface

A stated goal of the White House's *National Space Policy of the United States of America* is to increase the resilience of mission-essential functions enabled by space assets and their supporting infrastructure against disruption, degradation, and destruction.[1] Enhancing the resilience of U.S. space capabilities, however, must occur in a financially constrained environment. In work conducted for the U.S. Air Force, the RAND Corporation developed a framework for identifying effective and economically feasible (i.e., excluding the space segment) measures for increasing the resilience of its space assets. As part of that effort, RAND researchers conducted a review of the academic literature and case-study reports and summaries that gathered information about how other organizations build resilient missions. This report summarizes key findings from this review that have broad application to any organization seeking to enhance resilience as well as specifically to the space community. This research was sponsored by the commander, Air Force Space Command, and was conducted within the Force Modernization and Employment Program of RAND Project AIR FORCE as part of a fiscal year 2014 project, "Space Resilience: Developing a Strategy for Balancing Capability and Affordability with Resilience." The information presented here is current as of September 2014.

RAND Project AIR FORCE

RAND Project AIR FORCE (PAF), a division of the RAND Corporation, is the U.S. Air Force's federally funded research and development center for studies and analyses. PAF provides the Air Force with independent analyses of policy alternatives affecting the development, employment, combat readiness, and support of current and future air, space, and cyber forces. Research is conducted in four programs: Force Modernization and Employment; Manpower, Personnel, and Training; Resource Management; and Strategy and Doctrine. The research reported here was prepared under contract FA7014-06-C-0001.

Additional information about PAF is available on our website:
www.rand.org/paf

This report documents work originally shared with the U.S. Air Force on September 23, 2014. The draft report, issued in November 2014, was reviewed by formal peer reviewers and U.S. Air Force subject-matter experts.

---

[1] White House, *National Space Policy of the United States of America*, Washington, D.C., June 28, 2010.

Table of Contents

Summary

Organizations—municipalities, critical public services (e.g., hospitals), and large businesses—develop plans for operating through, and post, a potential disaster to ensure capable operations over time in the face of adversarial action, financial constraints, and even weather. A review of the academic literature on *resilience* and related terms was conducted to determine how these entities define and assess resilience and prepare for, organize, and respond to a threat event. The results from this literature review yield insights and general guidance for assessing and building resilience. Specifically, the results from this review offer general insights that could be used by the Air Force space community to address resilience in a non-materiel manner. A general summary of how other communities address resilience is presented here; a more detailed discussion on how these general insights can provide more specific guidance to the Air Force is discussed in the main report for this project.[2]

Resilience, as presented in the literature, is an attribute of a system that generally indicates its ability to maintain critical operations in the face of adverse disruptions. Beyond this general definition lie many variances based on community characteristics, threat environments, and overall operational goals. Attributes, such as complexity, structure, training, and performance objectives, determine how a community approaches resilience, while characteristics of the operational environment, including risk tolerance, scope of possible threats, and expected impact, indicate which indicators are appropriate for assessing resilience. Different communities have therefore developed unique concepts of and approaches to resilience, along with appropriate corresponding indicators that then vary among communities. In the psychological community, resilience is demonstrated when an individual emerges from an adverse experience with increased psychological and emotional strength. The factors that make an individual psychologically resilient are often more subjective and attitude related, and here the primary resilience metric is the emotional well-being of the individual.[3] In contrast, engineers characterize a structure as resilient based on its ability to avoid failure; factors that contribute to structural resilience include physical strength and robustness, and the ability to avoid structural failure is the primary resilience metric.[4] In ecological communities, the ability to adapt to new threats enables resilience of the entire community, and this flexibility is an important metric in evaluating these systems.

---

[2] Gary McLeod, George Nacouzi, Paul Dryer, Mel Eisman, Myron Hura, Krista S. Langeland, David Manheim, and Geoffrey Torrington, *Enhancing Space Resilience Through Non-Materiel Means*, Santa Monica, Calif.: RAND Corporation, RR-1067-AF, 2016.

[3] *Psychology Today* online, "Resilience: All About Resilience," undated.

[4] Barbara J. Jennings, Eric D. Vugrin, and Deborah K. Belasich, "Resilience Certification for Commercial Buildings: A Study of Stakeholder Perspective," *Environment Systems and Decisions*, Vol. 33, 2013, pp. 184–194.

Based on these variances, enhancing resilience requires a varied approach that takes into account these community attributes and operational environment. This report presents the approaches taken by three different types of communities to develop and maintain resilient operations. The discussion presented in this report illustrates methods for building resilience through withstanding an adverse event (impact avoidance and robustness), resilience through adaptation and flexibility, and resilience through recovery and restoration. Communities seeking to develop more resilient operations can gain insight from the academic studies and experience provided in the literature. By identifying the methods and lessons derived from previous studies of similar operational environments and how they addressed resilience, similar operations can benefit from this insight. These approaches are broadly described in this report as: *withstand*, *adapt*, and *recover*. Recognizing that any given organization will incorporate all three of these approaches in an overall resilience plan, this report seeks to highlight organizations that will be most likely to emphasize one of these approaches over another.

General Approaches for Building Resilient Operations

Impact Avoidance

Communities that have a low tolerance for risk or failure seek to withstand a potential degradation or disruption by avoiding impact entirely. These *hazardous* industries include, for example, air traffic control and nuclear power plant management. Hazardous industries are characterized by their unforgiving environment and severe consequences for mission failure,[56] and the resilience of a hazardous industry is determined by its ability to avoid degradation. This depends on its reliability or robustness when the mission being considered cannot tolerate any degradation, error, or failure.[7] These organizations often prioritize performance above, for example, profitability, timeliness, and efficiency.

Error reporting is a vital aspect of resilience in these organizations. These types of organizations cannot rely on trial and error to boost resilience due to the high cost of error, but *can* increase resilience by focusing on and learning from failure and near misses. In addition, a full understanding of risk and sources of these errors is also a key objective for hazardous industries. While developing a complete understanding of the full range of risks is an intractable goal, and hardening against the highly improbable may be cost prohibitive, emphasizing an understanding of the *highest impact* risks is particularly important for hazardous organizations.

---

[5] Karl E. Weick, Kathleen M. Sutcliffe, and David Obstfeld, "Organizing for High Reliability: Processes of Collective Mindfulness," in R.S. Sutton and B. M. Staw, eds., *Research in Organizational Behavior*, Vol. 1, Stanford, Calif.: Jai Press, 1999, pp. 81–123.

[6] Todd R. LaPorte, "High Reliability Organizations: Unlikely, Demanding, and At Risk," *Journal of Contingencies and Crisis Management*, Vol. 4, No. 2, June 1996, pp. 60–71.

[7] Karlene H. Roberts, "Some Characteristics of One Type of High Reliability Organization," *Organization Science*, Vol. 1, No. 2, 1990, pp. 160.

A culture of communication and collaboration also significantly contributes to the robustness of high-reliability organizations (HROs). Collaboration requires reliable communication infrastructure that includes a clear reporting system, allows appropriate information flow, and facilitates shared mission awareness and shared mission goals. In addition, the skills and ability of personnel to make decisions is especially important in the high-risk environment discussed here. Personnel with detailed technical knowledge of the systems being used will be more adept at identifying potential mitigations when threatened with potential performance degradation or failure. Due to the high level of integration between these systems, however, personnel must also have general background and knowledge of these systems to ensure flexibility during emergency operations. Successful HROs find a balance between these seemingly paradoxical requirements.

Adaptation and Flexibility

Adaptation is the most appropriate approach for those industries that have more flexible tolerances for small disruptions. These industries prioritize the ability to operate through changes and disruptions, maintaining critical capabilities during and after a disruption. The primary metric for these industries is flexibility, or the ability to evolve to accommodate changing circumstances. Business operations that require continuous operations in a dynamic environment exemplify this approach toward resilience, one that seeks a balance between efficiency and reliability, and our review references literature on business management and operations to determine how these organizations support resilience through flexibility.

One important method for achieving resilience in these organizations is implementing measures to increase information availability to those who are able to synthesize and use it. Not only does increased visibility expedite the detection of potential disruptions and enable impact mitigation from these disruptions as they occur, but this increased situational awareness facilitates the identification of inefficiencies in the overall process. The increase in information made available to personnel, however, needs to be balanced with the ability of the personnel to ingest this information. A flood of information will not likely prove to be useful and could even damage resilience efforts, so a balance must be achieved.

Designing processes and operations for flexibility is another key method for building resilience and is enabled by increased sharing of information. This method entails the development of a proactive risk-management strategy that requires a dynamic assessment of possible exposure to circumstances that could impact capability.[8,9] By redesigning processes with

---

[8] Maria Jesús Sáenz and Elena Revilla, "Creating More Resilient Supply Chains," *MIT Sloan Management Review*, Summer 2014.

[9] Kelly Marchese and Jerry O'Dwyer, "From Risk to Resilience: Using Analytics and Visualization to Reduce Supply Chain Vulnerability," *Deloitte Review*, Issue 14, January 17, 2014.

responsiveness and flexibility in mind, it is possible to build a dynamic culture that is able to respond more effectively.[10]

Successful business practices, and supply chains in particular, achieve a balance between reducing vulnerability and maintaining efficient operations by using these above approaches. The flexibility afforded through information flow, shared mission awareness, and processes that were redesigned with flexibility and adaptability in mind is key to mission resilience for a dynamic environment characterized by moderate risk.

Recovery and Restoration

In contrast to HROs that strive to be failure resistant and business supply chains that are intended to operate through threat scenarios, some communities with high-priority missions instead emphasize the enabling of rapid recovery immediately following impact rather than avoiding or accommodating this impact. The reasons for this may include the degree of difficulty and expense required for hardening the organization to all possible threats, the large number of possible impacts that would need to be anticipated in order to avoid impact, and the sheer number of facilities that would need to be hardened to secure the entire system. In the wake of a disrupting event with high impact, such as a natural disaster, some high-priority communities strive for rapid recovery of mission-critical capabilities even as they follow procedures to minimize impact.

Recovery operations can involve both evacuation to alternate facilities and the restoration of current infrastructure/facilities. For the first approach, evacuation procedures in response to a threat event, full-scale exercises conducted prior to threat impact can reveal more efficient methods and time-saving measures that can be incorporated into a periodically edited emergency response plan.[11] Incorporating lessons learned from response-planning exercises can significantly increase the efficiency and efficacy of future response efforts. The second approach is repairing and restoring infrastructure. During disaster response, time is critical, and the speed with which the source of the failure can be identified and addressed is the primary metric for resilience. Having experienced personnel on call, supporting shared mission awareness among all personnel, and establishing coordinated reporting procedures can minimize response times during an emergency.[12]

---

[10] Yossi Sheffi, "Building a Resilient Supply Chain," *Harvard Business Review Supply Chain Strategy* newsletter, Vol. 1, No. 8, October 2005.

[11] Christina Verni, "A Hospital System's Response to a Hurricane Offers Lessons, Including the Need for Mandatory Interfacility Drills," *Health Affairs*, Vol. 31, No. 8, 2012, pp. 1841–1821.

[12] James Pat Smith and Gulfport CARRI team, "Organizational Resilience: Mississippi Power as a Case Study," *A Gulfport Resilience Essay of the Community and Regional Resilience Institute,* March 2013.

General Practices for Building Resilience

Each of the concepts presented above provides some specific insight into methods for ensuring resilience for different mission goals: avoid risk, operate through, and recover. Hazardous industries in particular may significantly increase resilience by learning from errors and developing detailed yet dynamic response plans. Supply-chain management seeks to develop resilience through enhanced situational awareness and disaggregated and flexible decisionmaking. Recovery operations often can improve resilience through incorporating lessons from testing and exercises and assuring availability of skilled personnel on call. These specific concepts can provide some guidance tailored for a particular industry type or mission objective. Yet while each of these approaches to resilience may use unique practices and methods, common themes were repeated throughout the literature. These shared themes in particular may offer guidance for increasing resilience in the diverse and complex space community.

Common Themes

Information sharing and shared awareness of mission will increase the efficiency and effectiveness of operations both during and following a threat event. Implementing organizational structures and building internal cultures that support and encourage information flow and situation awareness are shown in the literature and case-study reports to optimize operations and personnel performance during and following a threat event or disruption.

Clear reporting structures and cultures that support error reporting will allow an organization to develop more resilient operations by incorporating lessons from previous errors. Information flow is supported by a clear reporting structure that not only supports integrated communication, but also builds accountability. Establishing well-defined reporting procedures is shown to maximize the efficiency and timeliness of operations in each mission type discussed here, and developing a culture that supports the reporting of failures and near misses is a key element of this reporting structure.

Appropriate balance between flexible personnel with distributed decisionmaking and specialized personnel with centralized decisionmaking. The ability to act outside of established response plans is key to building general resilience against unanticipated threats and impacts. Qualified personnel will have the ability to adapt responses in real time, and this ability needs to be accompanied by appropriate decisionmaking authority. Disaggregation of this authority during a threat response will enable swift response and action.

Accurate risk-assessment methods will facilitate better design and planning. While the full spectrum of possible impacts and risks may be impossible to capture, an accurate assessment of risk and failure tolerance will facilitate resource allocation and investment decisions.

Training for specific threats while maintaining flexibility in response procedures is a challenge, but meeting this challenge will allow an organization to address both specific and general threats. Developing appropriate training programs is a crucial to ensuring effective response to a threat event, and detailed exercises that address specific and known threats are crucial. Unanticipated threats, however, require personnel flexibility to respond outside of programmed procedures, and this presents a paradoxical challenge to operational managers, requiring compromise between efficient day-to-day operations and maximizing flexibility for disaster response.

Conclusion

The techniques presented in this literature review are intended to facilitate the identification of appropriate steps that a variety of organizations and communities, including the Air Force, could take to increase their resilience, particularly with limited resources. The lessons learned are not intended to be comprehensive, but instead provide some general guidelines for optimizing resource investment while assuring continued and successful operations. An organization can identify which of these measures summarized here are most appropriate and accessible based on resource availability, expected threats, organizational and operational restrictions, and mission requirements. Implementing these measures may allow these organizations to take significant steps toward sustaining mission-critical capabilities.

Acknowledgments

We would like to thank the project's action officer, Lt Col Steve Lindemuth, chief, Architectures and Support Branch, Air Force Space Command (AFSPC/A5XA), for his assistance during the course of the project. This work benefited greatly from extensive discussions with RAND colleagues Myron Hura, Paul Dreyer, and Lara Schmidt on the subject of resilience. We specifically acknowledge RAND colleague Laura Werber for her invaluable guidance in identifying references and key concepts in the academic literature. We also recognize the support and insightful contributions from Air Force fellows at RAND during this project, Col Andrew Kleckner, Lt Col Rose Jourdan, and Col Charles Galbreath. Finally, we would also like to thank RAND colleagues Anita Chandra, Don Snyder, and Timothy Vogus for their thoughtful and thorough reviews of the draft report. The content and recommendations of this report, however, remain the responsibility of the authors.

Abbreviations

FEMA	Federal Emergency Management Agency
HRO	high-reliability organization
IAEA	International Atomic Energy Agency
TEPCO	Tokyo Electric Power Company
NDRF	National Disaster Recovery Framework
SCRLC	Supply Chain Risk Leadership Council

1. Introduction

Background

Resilience is an indication of the ability of a system, architecture, or organization to meet the operating objective by maintaining or recovering critical capabilities when under attack, stressed, or otherwise compromised. Ensuring resilience can be a costly endeavor, and in a financially constrained environment, innovative approaches for assuring this resilience are required. Often, these innovative approaches lead to modifications of non-materiel aspects of a system or organization; such aspects include emergency response planning, organizational culture or structure, and training.

As part of a broader effort to develop a framework for assessing and enhancing the resilience of the Air Force space systems through non-materiel means, RAND researchers conducted a review of open-source literature with the goal of identifying some general methods and approaches used by other communities that face a similar challenge of achieving mission assurance and striving toward resilience with limited resources. The summary of this literature review illustrates some available options for communities (in particular, the U.S. space community) that are pursuing a higher level of resilience for their individual systems, organizations, or overall mission. The summary of this literature was then used in conjunction with interviews, discussions, and other research into specific Air Force needs; specific recommendations for the Air Force build from this literature review and are outlined in detail in the body of the main report for the broader effort. Observations and recommendations from this report contributed to and are represented in the main report for this project.[13]

Research Scope and Objective

Enhancing resilience has been discussed in a variety of conceptual and substantive ways, but clear guidelines for the types of approaches that may be applicable across domains are less common. Much has been written in academia about resilient system characteristics, and this research has examined a portion of this literature to gather lessons learned from academic experts and case-study reports. By examining key issues in the civilian community and identifying common traits, the Air Force space community could benefit from lessons learned from academic studies and previous experience in these civilian organizations. This review enabled the identification of key themes in building resilience and an understanding of the breadth of this concept. The report summarizes important features gathered from the academic literature review, and the objective of this report is to present defining characteristics of resilient mission

---

[13] McLeod et al., 2016.

operations, illustrate these characteristics with relevant case studies, and discuss general observations and themes that emerge from this literature.

Various organizations face similar needs for resilience and often turn to different general methods for achieving this resilience under resource constraints, in a variety of areas. Hospitals impacted by flooding need to, for example, rely on personnel capabilities to either continue operations in a compromised facility or to rely on training and exercises that facilitate effective evacuation procedures. Businesses need to develop contingency plans for supply-chain interruptions and shifting markets. In all of these cases, there are general lessons to be learned about how resilience can be achieved.

Research Approach

The scope of this literature review is intended to be strategic and targeted, with the goal of presenting an overview of prominent ideas in academia that could have bearing on studies that examine methods and techniques for increasing resilience in a variety of complex systems that may be evaluated, with the goal of increasing resilience. It is not a comprehensive review of resilience as it is understood and applied across the diverse and growing set of domains in which it is used; rather, this is an overview of specific concepts that have direct applicability to specific mission types.

The method used to identify important references for this literature review was multifaceted. The literature search emphasized publications on overall resilience, robustness, risk management, and recovery, as well as more targeted searches for case studies and literature on hazardous industries, supply-chain management, and disaster recovery. Based on journal reputation, citation counts, and applicability of content, we built a bibliography of key documents that discuss methods used by various types of organizations to build and maintain resilience. This bibliography reflects several significant threads in the discussion of resilience, and to further examine these threads, we selected a few case studies and collected literature on these events to determine their approach to resilience and identify successes and failures.

The case studies selected are intended to highlight specific types of communities and how they approach resilience: the first case study examines the hazardous industry community, the second examines the business supply-chain community, and the third examines utility companies and hospital resilience. Again, this list is not comprehensive, and the lessons learned from the cases included are not mutually exclusive. Despite the overlap, the cases each contain unique procedures and protocols that could provide important lessons to other communities seeking to improve their resilience, either by a successful demonstration of resilience or by learning from what did not work

The academic literature often addresses issues related to resilience with other associated terms and concepts. Therefore, we expanded the vocabulary in our study of resilience to include other key concepts and common terms that are closely associated with resilience; these concepts and terms include high-reliability organizations, robust design, and complex adaptive systems. We have tried to situate the discussion of each of these aspects properly in the context of resilience writ large. To do so, this report discusses three unique approaches to resilience and characterizes organizations that demonstrate resilient operations in each. Each chapter discusses one of these categories, defines mission characteristics unique to this community, presents academic findings related to resilience in these areas, and demonstrates these and other findings via brief summaries of case study reports. This report summarizes recurring themes from each segment to facilitate the identification of common attributes, resources, practices, and preparations shared by resilient organizations.

Report Structure

Chapter Two presents an overall view of resilience definitions and assessment indicators and methods, and then introduces the discussion of how different communities and industries require different approaches for building resilient operations. Subsequent chapters discuss different communities in more detail to distinguish between these approaches. Specifically, Chapter Three discusses hazardous industries and how they withstand and avoid impact due to the high risk associated with even small degradations in performance. Chapter Four discusses how businesses ensure that they can operate through a threat through strategic supply chain management, and Chapter Five provides a brief discussion and examples of recovery efforts following impact and system failures. Each chapter highlights a specific component of resilience and presents examples and discussion of best practices and lessons learned. A summary of the lessons learned from each distinct community, as well as general themes and insights, is presented in Chapter Six. The utility of this literature report is to enable the reader to identify applicable lessons that are most appropriate for a specific mission or organization, depending on mission type and threat environment and based on real world insights and academic findings.

2. Definitions, Characteristics, and Assessments of Resilience

Definitions of *Resilience*

Drawing on terminology from ecology and sociology, *resilience* is defined as "the capacity of a system, enterprise, or person to maintain its core purpose and integrity in the face of dramatically changed circumstances."[14] This general definition finds expression in a variety of specific contexts, and each of these contexts provides insight for developing resilient systems and organizations generally.

In the psychological community, resilience is a quality that allows an individual to recover from adversity stronger than before. The factors that make an individual psychologically resilient are often emotional and attitude related; here the primary resilience metric is the emotional well-being of the individual.[15] In contrast, engineers characterize a structure as resilient based on its ability to avoid failure; factors that contribute to structural resilience include physical strength and robustness or "the ability of a structure (or part of it) to withstand events (like fire, explosion, impact) or consequences of human errors, without being damaged to an extent disproportionate to the original cause."[16] In this approach to resilience, the ability to avoid structural failure is the primary metric.[17] In ecological communities, the ability to adapt to new threats enables resilience of the entire community, and this flexibility is an important metric in evaluating these systems. Inverse of the engineering definition, the ability to withstand is even presented as a concept outside of resilience. Political scientist Aaron Wildavsky, a political scientist known for his pioneering work on risk management in public policy, introduces an overall strategy of coping with risk by striking a balance between anticipation and resilience.[18] In his work, Wildavsky asserts that anticipation requires prediction and "specialized protection." Resilience, in contrast, relies on trial and error and the development of general capacities. This report includes anticipation as an element of resilience, rather than a separate concept, to emphasize that the goal of resilience is to maintain mission effectiveness, and achieving this goal by avoiding degradation represents one type of approach to resilience. This concept is illustrated further in the discussion of specific versus general resilience later in this section.

---

[14] Andrew Zolli and Ann Marie Healy, *Resilience: Why Things Bounce Back*, New York: Simon and Schuster, Inc., 2012, p. 7.

[15] *Psychology Today*, undated.

[16] Definition from engineering standard ISO 22111. See International Organization for Standardization (ISO), "Bases for Design of Structures—General Requirements," ISO 22111:2007, undated.

[17] Jennings, Vugrin, and Belasich, 2013.

[18] Aaron B. Wildavsky, *Searching for Safety*, Piscataway, N.J.: Transaction Publishers, 1988.

Each of these communities above represents a different mission type, and a widely varied definition of and approach to resilience, but in all examples, components can fail without compromising the core purpose and integrity of the overall organization. We define resilience for the purpose of this report, then as the ability to maintain a critical level of operational capability despite disruptive events and regardless of the impact on individual systems and components.[19]

Resilience Characteristics

Resilience is measured by the likelihood of mission assurance during and following a threat event and can be influenced by a variety of factors. Non-materiel factors that have the potential to enhance resilience are especially important in a constrained fiscal environment or if required technological capabilities are not feasible. In fact, non-materiel approaches to enhancing resilience may even be more effective. In some circumstances, developing a culture and strategy for resilience can have a higher impact than engineering for resilience.[20] The characteristics of a system that indicate its resilience vary from community to community, as discussed above. Shared indicators for resilience include adequacy of resources, level of knowledge and skills; level of diversity, information sharing, and number of leaders.[21] However, different communities have additional requirements that necessitate different indicators for evaluation.[22] In ecological systems, flexibility is prioritized, and resilience is often characterized in ecological systems as adaptive capacity.[23] In contrast, the resilience of physical, engineered systems is most often an indication of an ability to withstand physical forces without deformation, malfunction, or breaking; is measured by hardness or robustness; and requires planning for the worst-case scenario, with the understanding that design for worst-case scenarios protects against lesser forces.[24] In behavioral science, where people are subject to stresses that require not just resistance but adaptation and response, resilience is a term often used to describe the capability of a system or organism to bounce back following adversity, in addition to the measurement of

---

[19] Gen William Shelton, then commander of Air Force Space Command, defined *resilience* as "the ability of a system architecture to continue providing required capabilities in the face of system failures, environmental challenges, or adversary actions." See Air Force Space Command, "Resiliency and Disaggregated Space Architectures," white paper, Peterson AFB, Colo., undated (released August 21, 2013), p. 4

[20] Alan D. Meyer, "Adapting to Environmental Jolts," *Administrative Science Quarterly*, Vol. 27, No. 4, December 1982, pp. 515–537.

[21] Nabin Baral, "What Makes Grassroots Conservation Organizations Resilient? An Empirical Analysis of Diversity, Organizational Memory, and the Number of Leaders," *Environmental Management*, Vol. 51, No. 3, March 2013, pp. 738–749.

[22] Timothy J. Vogus and Kathleen M. Sutcliffe, "Organizational Resilience: Towards a Theory and Research Agenda," *ISIC IEEE Conference on Systems, Man, and Cybernetics*, October 2007, pp. 3418–3422.

[23] Steve Carpenter Brian Walker, J. Marty Anderies, and Nick Abel, "From Metaphor to Measurement: Resilience of What to What?" *Ecosystems*, Vol. 4, No. 8, December 2001, pp. 765–781.

[24] J. Park, T. P. Seager, P. S. C. Rao, M. Convertino, and I. Linkov, "Integrating Risk and Resilience Approaches to Catastrophe Management in Engineering Systems," *Risk Analysis*, Vol. 33, No. 3, 2013, pp. 356–367.

its capacity and time to recover.[25] Developing indicators for assessing resilience is challenged by this variability, but at the same time it is critical to incorporate each type of resilience into the assessment of the system as a whole. This will enable a multilevel view of resilience.

Resilience is further categorized by *specific* versus *general* indicators, presenting further challenges to developing universal indicators for this concept. *Specific resilience* refers to the capability to maintain mission functions during and following a specific threat or other event. *General resilience* is a measure of the ability to maintain operations over a range of unanticipated threats and events.[26] The assessment of mission assurance therefore requires clarification of which type of resilience is being evaluated. A system specifically tailored to resist the impact of a power outage, for example, may be poorly designed to withstand an earthquake. The system has *specific resilience*, but not *general resilience*. Ideally, the actions taken to increase specific resilience are able to increase general resilience as well, but this is not necessarily the case. Actions taken in response to a threat event, or in anticipation of it, can result in an incrementally changing system to accommodate the threat, or any other abrupt and significant alteration in system operations. In this way, resilience can be adaptive or transformative because, despite the risks, "sudden changes are ambiguous events that also benefit organizations."[27]

Resilience Assessment

Given the complexity of assessing the various qualitative and quantitative aspects of resilience, it is important to have a rigorous method for evaluating the systems. The task of fully modeling all aspects of a system against all possible risks to each would be an extremely difficult and expensive process. Skill, diversity, or the hardness of a physical substance is each an example of a characteristic that can be used to indicate resilience. Skill indicates the learned ability of an operator to use equipment, or the overall expertise and capabilities of a population to respond to a threat event. Diversity indicates the variability of features that may be impacted by such a threat event; if the threat specifically attacks one species, type of equipment, or physical attribute, then diversity in each of these will provide increased resilience to this threat. Hardness indicates the ability to withstand a threat event without catastrophic impact. Each of these indicators is measured using very different methods and with varying levels of subjectivity. In reality, almost all systems depend on components that have resilience that can be measured in disparate ways. Because of this, the evaluation of the overall resilience of the system requires an assessment of the resilience of its individual components and how each component interacts

---

[25] George A. Bonanno, "Loss, Trauma, and Human Resilience: Have We Underestimated the Human Capacity to Thrive After Extremely Aversive Events?" *American Psychologist*, Vol. 59, No. January 2004, pp. 20–28.

[26] Baral, 2013.

[27] Baral, 2013, and Meyer, 1982.

within the system. Several models exist for assessing resilience, and while the objective of this report is not to recommend a specific model, this section provides one example of how component and system resilience can be assessed. Further details on assessing resilience in the Air Force space community can be found in the main publication to emerge from this project work.[28]

A good model for resilience assessment will provide a clear set of indicators that enable insight into the level of resilience of different aspects of the system and appropriately integrate these components. One approach is to define sub-indicators for each component, such as maturity, as exemplified by the Supply Chain Risk Leadership Council's (SCRLC's) Maturity Model.[29] This example includes a maturity assessment that addresses event likelihood and consequence, albeit in a qualitative manner. For example, it is considered stage one (reactive) if there is "no formal process for analyzing likelihood and consequence to determine level of risk." It is stage three (proactive) if there is a "formal risk analysis process in place for analyzing internal likelihood and consequence based upon risk criteria to determine level of risk utilized." Best, if it is stage five (resilient), the company has a "comprehensive documented and integrated process for analyzing likelihood and consequence to determine level of risk across the enterprise and supply chain." This approach addresses specific resilience, since it requires evaluation of a known threat, and extension to general resilience is assumed if these same measures enhance the ability to face unanticipated threats as well. These descriptions allow for a clear gradation of the risk readiness, a concept often directly associated with resilience.

This idea of risk readiness is developed in the "dynamic safety" model described by Rasmussen and Cook in 2005.[30] This model describes a safe operating envelope that provides a volume, rather than a defined point, in which a system can safely operate. This approach highlights the trade-offs between risks of one type against risks of another type. An organization could adapt its behavior to address one risk, only to find itself at a higher risk from another threat at the opposite boundary. The overall operating space between where an organization is operating and the boundary of its safe operation is its safe operating envelope, and assessing the volume of this space by examining multiple risks in relationship to current operating parameters could be an insightful indicator of resilience.

These examples are only two of numerous frameworks for assessing resilience of systems and system components. As is evident in the case-study examples presented in this report, different indicators will be emphasized based on the overall mission goal. This will drive the development of an appropriate model for assessment.

---

[28] McLeod et al., 2016.

[29] Supply Chain Risk Leadership Council, "SCRLC Emerging Risks in the Supply Chain 2013," white paper, 2013a.

[30] R. Cook and J. Rasmussen, "Going Solid: A Model of System Dynamics and Consequences for Patient Safety," *Quality and Safety in Health Care*, Vol. 14, 2005, pp. 130–134.

Approaches to Building Resilience

Resilient systems and organizations often take varying approaches to mitigating risk and preparing for threats; for example, they may resist impact, adapt during an impact, or regain functionality after impact.[31] Resilience can then be categorized by these approaches: impact mitigation, real-time adaptation or response, and recovery efforts.[32] All three of these functions contribute to the overall resilience of the system, and appropriate measures to increase resilience may include aspects of each.

Impact mitigation is a key method for the system or organization to maintain operational capacity. This type of robustness is often a physical trait and usually is achieved by providing excess capacity. Facilities hardening and redundant communication systems can both provide robustness to a system or organization by allowing the system to absorb damage and minimize the lost capacity.

Real-time adaptation or response allows a system to operate through a disruptive event by adjusting its operations. The real-time response to a disruption characterizes the ability to adapt to incremental or sudden loss of capability by establishing alternate means to achieve this capability or to develop a way to maintain functionality without this capability. Here, instead of excess capacity, an organization relies on flexibility and easily replaceable sub-capabilities.

Recovery efforts include those activities following an impact for regaining mission-critical capability. In the event of a low-impact threat, an organization may maintain mission capability by operating through with minor adaptations. In a high-impact event, however, a mission capability can only be maintained by hardening to avoid impact altogether or ensuring a rapid and sufficient recovery following impact.

To address each of these types of resilience requirement areas, this report highlights key terms and concepts in the literature, along with several case studies, that demonstrate general wisdom and lessons learned for each case. The collected information will demonstrate key features of successful methods for ensuring mission success in each. The following table summarizes each of these three general approaches to resilience. This report discusses important features of each approach separately, yet organizations may often use aspects of all three of these approaches in combination, depending on their operational environment, risk aversions, and details of the mission.

---

[31] Meyer, 1982.

[32] White House, 2010; U.S. Department of Homeland Security, "National Preparedness Guidelines," updated August 15, 2015.

Table 1. Comparison of Types of Resilience Efforts

Withstand	Adapt	Recover
Goal: avoid impact from threat without losing capability	Goal: operate through a threat while losing minimal capability	Goal: minimize down time after impact and loss of capability
Characterized by robustness, redundancy, hardness	Characterized by flexibility in operations, development of alternate capabilities	Characterized by reaction capabilities and speed

3. Withstand: Hazardous Industries

Unique Traits and Challenges of Hazardous Industries

When the price of degradation or failure is exceptionally high, mission resilience requires the ability to withstand a disruption without significant reduction of capabilities. A reduction in capabilities would represent in many cases a significant safety hazard. These hazardous industries are characterized by their unforgiving environment and severe consequences for failure of operational safety measures,[33] and the resilience of a hazardous industry is determined by its reliability or robustness when degradation, error, or failure cannot be tolerated.[34] Some examples of hazardous organizations include air-traffic control and nuclear power plants. Air-traffic control has a low tolerance for collision, and as such may prioritize collision avoidance over, for example, cost-cutting measures or timeliness. Similarly, a nuclear power plant may prioritize measures that mitigate the risk of a meltdown, even if this significantly increases operations costs. Any hazardous organization should prioritize error avoidance above, for example, factors such as performance, profitability, timeliness, and efficiency. Hazardous organizations with appropriate priorities that demonstrate nearly error-free operations over a significant period of time are referred to as High-Reliability Organizations (HROs).[35] HROs are a subset of organizations operating in hazardous industries and are distinguished by their "highly hazardous, low risk performance as a condition of delivering their benefits."[36] Practices undertaken by the HROs may provide insight on best approaches for avoiding significant impact on critical operations during a threat event.

One important characteristic challenge faced by hazardous industries is their inability to rely on trial and error to incrementally improve resilience. In industries with a higher tolerance for degradation, attention often is more focused on "success rather than failure and efficiency rather than reliability."[37] In contrast, hazardous industries need to pay special attention to the potential causes of failure and eschew efficiency in favor of reliability.[38] HROs will, for example, analyze possible causes following a near-miss or failure event and use it as a learning opportunity. A successful HRO will encourage operator reporting of near misses, along with any safety concerns or errors. In health care, another industry where the risk for failure can be extremely high in

---

[33] Weick, Sutcliffe, and Obstfeld, 1999.

[34] Roberts, 1990.

[35] E.g., Roberts, 1990.

[36] LaPorte, 1996.

[37] Weick, Sutcliffe, and Obstfeld, 1999.

[38] Karl E. Weick, "Organizational Culture as a Source of High Reliability," *California Management Review*, Vol. 29, No. 2, Winter 1987, pp. 112–127.

some circumstances, error reporting is heavily emphasized as a goal for increasing reliability, though one that perhaps is yet to be obtained.[39] When accidents do occur, when threats are reevaluated, or when potential sources or error are identified, HROs engage in adaptive learning by addressing these failures and modifying a dynamic response plan. In this way, HROs see failure as a way to enhance resilience in a manner that is fundamentally different than a nonhazardous industry, which can afford to test and learn continuously.[40] This culture of error reporting and learning from near misses increases organization-wide situational awareness and is characterized in Weick, Sutcliffe, and Obstfeld as "collective mindfulness" that emphasizes not only observation of potential errors and near misses but also subsequent action based on these observations; this is presented as a key contributor to the success of HROs.[41]

Challenges from Complexity and Tight Integration

Complex, integrated systems are often a hallmark of hazardous industries, compounding the challenge of developing means of avoiding disruption and degradation. These elevated levels of complexity and integration are attributed to the use of advanced technology, extensive command and control requirements, and sheer size,[42] and these traits present a formidable challenge to ensure resilient operations. Indeed, the most thorough preparations, training, and organizational structure may not be sufficient to overcome the potential for system failure.[43] The assumption here is that the organization has chosen to accept this risk and now has the objective of identifying ways to mitigate this risk as much as possible.

One challenge is the development of appropriate testing and exercises to evaluate and ensure reliability; the systems used for these operations are often too complex and intricately integrated to allow a full-scale model to be built for full operational testing, an otherwise valuable method for identifying sources of potential error in real-time operations. Compounded with this challenge to testing is the risk that even minor errors can be catastrophic in real operations. While a drop in business due to ill-timed marketing can be corrected for a retail business, catastrophe resulting from a miscalculation in air-traffic control, for instance, can cause fatal accidents. A second challenge is that these very characteristics that inhibit testing and

---

[39] Linda T. Kohn, Janet M. Corrigan, and Molla S. Donaldson, eds., *To Err is Human: Building a Safer Health System*, Washington, D.C.: National Academies Press, 2000; Joel S. Weissman, Catherine L. Annas, Arnold M. Epstein, Eric C. Schneider, Brian Clarridge, Leslie Kirle, Constantine Gatsonis, Sandra Feibelmann, and Nancy Ridley, "Error Reporting and Disclosure Systems: Views from Hospital Leaders," *Journal of the American Medical Association*, Vol. 293, No. 11, March 16, 2005, pp. 1359–1366; Zane Robinson, and Ronda G. Hughes, "Error Reporting and Disclosure," in Ronda G. Hughes, ed., *Patient Safety and Quality: An Evidence-Based Handbook for Nurses*, Rockville, Md.: Agency for Healthcare Research and Quality, 2008, chapter 35.

[40] Weick, Sutcliffe, and Obstfeld, 1999.

[41] Weick, Sutcliffe, and Obstfeld, 1999.

[42] Roberts, 1990, and Charles Perrow, *Normal Accidents: Living with High-Risk Technologies*, updated edition, Princeton, N.J.: Princeton University Press, 1999.

[43] Perrow, 1984.

verification, complexity and tight integration of operations, actually increase the potential for error.[44] This complexity decreases information flow and visibility while increasing the likelihood of accidents and errors.[45] This idea is discussed in the literature via the concept of *requisite variety* mismatch.[46] Both the system and its operators require a comparable level of complexity for optimum operations, but if the complexity of the system or organization under consideration exceeds the complexity of the operators, this tends to degrade the reliability by introducing error potential.[47]

Approaches for Enhancing Robustness in a Highly Complex Environment

HROs are those hazardous organizations that successfully demonstrate reliability over time, despite the challenges often faced from complexity and tight integration. While recognizing the high potential for error, HROs emphasize measures that can minimize these errors and thereby enhance the ability of a system to withstand a disruption without catastrophic failure. Several methods for increasing this robustness are presented and discussed in the academic literature.[48] Two measures in particular are non-materiel in nature and are concepts that can be applied without relying on increased engineering, development of new technology, or increased automation. These measures are *enhanced training* and *optimized organizational structure*.

Extensive training on technologically complex systems cannot insulate the system from possible failure, but taking these measures would decrease the likelihood of failure and increase the likelihood that the operator could recognize and mitigate small errors before they become catastrophic. An ideal, albeit unachievable, training program would provide extensive technological training for each system component as well as training for each possible failure mode. More extensive training in general would more easily allow operators to recognize compromises to system performance earlier. Increased quality control and the training that facilitates this can significantly increase the overall robustness of the system operations, though these measures alone are insufficient to ensure that no accidents occur.[49] In his pioneering book on the subject, Charles Perrow recognizes that while fully developing a comprehensive portfolio of possible failure modes is untenable for even moderately complex systems, developing a more comprehensive training program to address as many permutations of these failure modes as possible will nevertheless improve overall robustness. Further, a comprehensive and thorough

---

[44] Weick, 1987; LaPorte, 1986; Perrow, 1984.

[45] Perrow, 1984.

[46] Walter Buckley, "Society as a Complex Adaptive System," in Walter Buckley, ed., *Modern Systems Research for the Behavioral Scientist*, Chicago, Ill.: Aldine Publishing Company, 1968, pp. 490–513.

[47] Weick, 1987.

[48] See, for example, Roberts, 1990, and Weick, 1987.

[49] Perrow, 1984.

training program that seeks to address the full spectrum of potential threat scenarios would, in principle, provide *specific* resilience, but not *general* resilience.

This general resilience can be better supported through optimizing aspects of the organizational structure. An organizational structure that encourages collaboration and shared mission awareness can enhance robustness; increased collaboration fosters teamwork in a way that allows for integration of efforts during an emergency.[50] This collaboration and flexibility will require a high level of information sharing as well as increased distribution of decisionmaking authority. When unforeseen threats occur, an organizational structure that supports collaboration will help ensure that personnel have sufficient knowledge of the operations to enable them to make these decisions and respond appropriately, even outside of trained procedures, in an unanticipated crisis.

This distribution of responsibility not only needs to be present, but also needs to be clear and concise. Well-defined hierarchical structures within an organization and clear lines of responsibility can play an important role in mitigating the negative effects of the complexity and integration inherent in many hazardous industries.[51] However, while clear lines of responsibility foster a sense of accountability accompanied by a low tolerance for failure,[52] this concept is often in conflict with personnel flexibility, again highlighting the potential conflict between specific and general resilience. Well-defined job functions support accountability, but granting personnel a degree of elasticity facilitates more rapid response in a crisis. HROs successfully avoid catastrophic impact by carefully balancing this flexibility and accountability in their personnel.

The often-paradoxical challenge between fixed response mechanisms for specific resilience and flexible response capabilities for general resilience again surfaces. Extensive and deep technological knowledge of specific systems will support specific resilience against known threats, but flexible personnel that have a broad understanding of general operations will better support resilience against unanticipated threats. A hazardous industry should carefully assess the balance between these two concepts when evaluating training and personnel programs as well as the distribution of responsibilities in the organization.

Both organization and training programs require this careful balance. Training programs should address both specific threats and responses while developing a general understanding of operations to enable response to general threats; these efforts may not always be complementary. Training can be divided into two elements to achieve this balance. The first element, *collaboration*, depends on teams who have "specific roles, perform interdependent tasks, are

---

[50] David P. Baker, Rachel Day, and Eduardo Salas, "Teamwork as an Essential Component of High Reliability Organizations," *Health Services Research*, Vol. 41, No. 4, Part II, August 2006, pp. 1576–1598.

[51] Roberts, 1990.

[52] Philip E. Tetlock, "Accountability: A Social Check on the Fundamental Attribution Error," *Social Psychology Quarterly*, Vol. 48, No. 3, September 1985, pp. 227–236.

adaptable, and share a common goal."[53] This element emphasizes the shared mission-awareness requirement for reliable operations as well as the adaptability of personnel actions. The second element is *taskwork* (e.g., surgical skill), and this component more closely addresses the personnel skill availability, knowledge, and background. Personnel should be both skilled and able to adapt, and shared mission awareness is imperative for reliable operations. Organizations should support collaboration and flexibility by providing the appropriate decisionmaking authority to personnel during an emergency. In general, unfortunately there is no specific guideline for how to best achieve this balance; the details of what this balance looks like are heavily dependent on a number of specific organizational characteristics, such as size, geographical distribution, and inherent complexity, as well as personnel characteristics, such as skill level and extent and type of training. Achieving this balance will require each organization to examine the role of each of these variables.

Case Study: Fukushima Daiichi Nuclear Disaster

A nuclear power plant illustrates operational procedures for an organization with high levels of risk and complexity and little tolerance for failure, and is therefore represents a hazardous industry. Lessons can be learned both from nuclear power plants' standard operating procedures and safety practices as well as from specific failures such as Fukushima in Japan. This particular case study of a nuclear power plant is used to illustrate two important issues faced by organizations that strive to harden themselves against the ultimate failure. The first issue is the virtual impossibility of hardening a highly complex system against all failure modes, regardless of the tolerance for risk. The second is the importance of including high-risk/low-likelihood events when examining resilience.

First, a review of the standard operating procedures is presented here to provide some context for this case study. The International Atomic Energy Association (IAEA) outlines the standard safety procedures for a nuclear power plant and emphasizes several key priorities. All activities that take place in the power plant that could impact operational safety have clear and explicit instructions. Beyond these established procedures, IAEA prioritizes training, reporting structures, and incorporation of feedback.[54] To ensure that operators have sufficient system-specific expertise, component manufacturers and reactor vendors should be brought in to provide comprehensive training when the plant is first brought online. In addition, personnel should be encouraged to report near misses and possible problems, and a clear reporting structure should be established. Similarly, feedback programs can facilitate the identification of potential problems and possible mitigation strategies. Establishing a systematic evaluation process when near misses

---

[53] Baker, Day, and Salas, 2006.

[54] International Atomic Energy Association, *The Operating Organization for Nuclear Power Plants, IAEA Safety Standards Series No. NS-G-2.4*, Vienna: International Atomic Energy Agency, 2011b.

occur is a vital element of this feedback component, and results from this evaluation process should be incorporated into future training procedures.[55]

Beyond design-basis accidents refer to events that are dismissed during the design process due to low perceived likelihood.[56] One such beyond design-basis accident occurred in March 2011, when a magnitude 9.0 earthquake Tōhoku earthquake triggered a tsunami that hit the Fukushima Daiichi nuclear power plant in Japan. Nuclear power plants are a representative hazardous industry due to their risk of catastrophic failure. The earthquake and resulting tsunami that disabled three of the six reactors at this plant illustrate the challenge hazardous industries face when designing systems and preparing personnel for potential threats.

Designing systems for a hazardous industry requires an accurate assessment of the risk boundaries. In 2002, the Tokyo Electric Power Company (TEPCO) evaluated the design-basis tsunami height to be around 5.5 meters.[57] The seawall for the plant was ten meters high, and while an internal report in 2008 warned TEPCO that the Fukushima plant could face tsunamis up to 10.2 meters high, the probability was assessed to be so unlikely that no action was taken to increase the height of the seawall.[58] The tsunami that hit Fukushima was estimated at around 14–15 meters high, demonstrating a beyond design-basis event. This example illustrates the importance in a high-risk operation of looking beyond the most likely impacts during the design. Within the confines of financial constraints and engineering capabilities, design of these systems should consider the maximum possible impact. While it is not likely practical to harden against this upper bound, these low likelihood/high impact scenarios cannot be as easily ignored, as they perhaps may be in a low-risk environment. When the stakes are low, the tails of the probability curve can be ignored. When the stakes are high, the tail should be an important element of the design considerations.

Preparing for possible threats also requires a consideration of a combination of incidents, not just the potential impact from an individual event. Due to the impact of the earthquake, all power lines from the grid to the power plant were destroyed, and communication capabilities were significantly degraded.[59] As a safety measure following the earthquake impact, all operating reactors were shut down, but these reactors still required cooling immediately following shutdown, as the accumulated radioactive material decayed.[60] These cooling systems require electricity, and since the plant was cut off from the grid, the system required the use of backup

---

[55] International Atomic Energy Association, 2011b.

[56] U.S. Nuclear Regulatory Commission, "Beyond Design-Basis Accidents," updated July 23, 2015.

[57] Masashi Hirano, Taisuke Yonomoto, Masahiro Ishigaki, Norio Watanabe, Yu Maruyama, Yasuteru Sibamoto, Tadashi Watanabe, and Kiyofumi Moriyama, "Insights from Review and Analysis of the Fukushima Dai-Ichi Accident," *Journal of Nuclear Science and Technology*, Vol. 49, No. 1, January 2012, pp. 1–17.

[58] Tokyo Electric Power Company, Inc. (TEPCO), "Fukushima Nuclear Accident Analysis Report," June 20, 2012.

[59] Hirano et al., 2012.

[60] James M. Acton and Mark Hibbs, "Why Fukushima Was Preventable," *Carnegie Endowment for International Peace,* March 6, 2012.

diesel generators. The subsequent tsunami, however, destroyed the seawater pumps required for the operation of these generators. Backup batteries provided a third level of redundancy, but the flooding from the tsunami destroyed these.[61] Reactor cooling now became impossible, and pressure inside the reactors built as cooling water evaporated, resulting in leaks that released a significant amount of radiation. The level of radiation released was catastrophic, requiring large-scale evacuation of the surrounding area and resulting in substantial death tolls from the effects of radiation.[62] As illustrated in this instance of one miscalculation escalating to the failure of the entire system, correlated risks and system interdependencies need to be carefully considered when evaluating resilience.

Summary: Hazardous Industries

Industries with catastrophic consequences for failure should have a different calculus for addressing resilience than those that can tolerate disruption. These industries cannot rely on trial and error to boost resilience, but can increase resilience by focusing on previous failure and near misses. To accomplish this, the organizational structure must support a culture that encourages reporting and communication. HROs are those hazardous industries that have demonstrated the ability to achieve reliability, and methods used by HROs to achieve reliability can be applied to improve any process that seeks to develop an assurance against mission capability degradation.[63]

Hazardous industries often view robustness as equivalent to resilience, and to achieve robustness a comprehensive understanding of risks should be the goal, albeit, in many cases, an unattainable one. A more comprehensive assessment of the full range of risks permits the organization to prepare for the worst, not the most probable; the Fukushima case study illustrates the dire consequences of an insufficient assessment. This type of preparation is especially challenging, since the worst-possible and least-likely scenario is probably the most expensive threat to address. Preparing for an unlikely scenario often needs to be balanced against other threats and priorities, and an enhanced understanding of the full spectrum of risks and threats will inform decisions on the most effective cost allocation.

In addition to accurate risk assessments, a culture of communication and collaboration significantly contributes to the robustness of an HRO. Collaboration requires reliable communication infrastructure that includes a clear reporting system, allows appropriate information flow, and facilitates shared mission awareness and shared mission goals. Ensuring a culture that encourages and supports the reporting of errors and near misses is essential. Further, the reporting of these errors needs to have a clear path toward action to incorporate lessons

---

[61] Acton and Hibbs, 2012.

[62] International Atomic Energy Association, "Report of Japanese Government to the IAEA Ministerial Conference on Nuclear Safety," June 2011a.

[63] Weick, 1987.

learned from these errors. "Learning . . . does not occur when an error is discovered. Learning occurs when the discovery or insight is followed by action."[64] Incorporating this information into future training and response plans is a key activity for building resilience in a high-risk environment. Coupled with this reporting system is a hierarchical structure with sharp lines of accountability, giving each party a shared responsibility for the mission objective.

The skills and ability of personnel to make decisions are especially important in the high-risk environment discussed here. Due to the complexity and interdependencies of the systems used in many configurations found in hazardous industries, personnel should receive training on specific systems and interfaces from the appropriate experts. In addition, due to the high level of integration between these systems, personnel must have the general background and knowledge required to engage in more flexible operations should an emergency occur. HROs find a balance between these seemingly paradoxical requirements. Overall, a prominent trait of HROs is reporting and learning from errors and near misses. A collaborative culture that adjusts dynamically to changing circumstances and new information facilitates learning from these events, while enabling shared mission awareness among all personnel. Resilience is, in this way, incorporated into the culture of an organization.

---

[64] Bertrand Moingeon and Amy Edmondson, eds., *Organizational Learning and Competitive Advantage*, London: Sage Publications, Ltd., 1996.

4. Adapt and Respond: Supply-Chain Risk Management

Characteristics of Supply-Chain Management and Risk Factors

While HROs prioritize reliability above all else, many business operations seek a balance between efficiency and reliability through strategic supply-chain development. Rather than withstanding a threat event by maintaining full capability throughout the duration of the threat, businesses often focus more on continuous adaptation to events in a manner that allows them to reduce operational disruption in a cost-effective manner. This chapter discusses resilience for organizations that have a high tolerance for risk, operate in a relatively consistent and predictable manner on a day-to-day basis, and have a large and consistent demand often strive for resilience. The case study presented here exhibits the importance of striking a balance between efficiency and resilience for such organizations. They must consider how to ensure longevity (through effective and efficient day-to-day operations), while also ensuring short-term viability (by developing the ability to operate through disruptions). Supply chains vividly illustrate the efforts of business to optimize efficiency while minimizing vulnerability.

After the adoption of *Kanban* (看板), or *just-in-time production*, by Toyota in the 1940s and 1950s[65] supply chains have been the focus of intensive reworking, at first for efficiency alone. When disrupted, the increased interconnectedness and efficiency of the supply chains of businesses can cause financial losses and significant problems in other parts of the business—making resilience a critical concern. The most important goal is to prevent the system from breaking and allow the business as a whole to "operate through" the various circumstances; adverse events, changing environments, or mistakes that would otherwise cascade.

Business has been at the forefront of developing organizational resilience techniques in the area of supply chains that were optimized for efficiency because these methods can help with minimizing losses due to unexpected events, without ignoring the goal of maximizing profits. A naïve cost-benefit analysis could suggest that any loss of operational efficiency is purely a cost, but more-thorough accounting reveals that there are many risks that are mitigated by more resilient supply chains. This is a clear case of where "every complex system requires trade-offs. [Businesses can trade] high efficiency for higher vulnerabilities."[66] As a result, risk management and resilience of supply chains has become a significant subfield of study, with dozens of articles and several books discussing how to perform risk management for supply chains, and how

---

[65] K. Sugimori, K. Kusunoki, F. Cho, and S. Uchikawa, "Toyota Production System and Kanban System: Materialization of Just-in-Time and Respect-for-Human System," *International Journal of Production Research*, Vol. 15, No. 6. 1977, pp. 553–564.

[66] Sáenz and Revilla, 2014.

supply-chain resilience can be achieved without sacrificing the operational efficiency that tightly connected supply chains achieve.

Approaches to Achieving Supply-Chain Resilience

As an initial step in any risk-management process, the risks to be managed must be assembled.[67] The SCRLC has produced best practices documents for Supply Chain Risk Management.[68] These documents include both how to develop a "risk register" of salient risks (Section 4), and a list of sample risks across many domains (Appendix 2.1). The SCRLC has also produced a document listing emerging risks as of 2013.[69] Despite these exhaustive lists, they advise "continual monitoring and review of risks and their treatment." This is because even a full risk-management process typically only is able to monitor risks that have been understood and quantified.

Views of Risks

Once the set of risks to monitor and plan for have been assembled, a critical task in enabling response is visibility. Many specific approaches to achieving this visibility have been suggested. A feature common in many of the approaches is to understand the system itself in order to be able to understand and respond to risks. "Complex supply chains require sophisticated, connected tools to monitor risks, predict disruptions, and support rapid recovery."[70] The first step, then, is to see what is happening in the system.

Deloitte, a consulting firm that has done significant work in the area, mentions supply-chain mapping, risk visualization, and risk indicators as the initial tools needed to understand the system. "Visibility is being able to track and monitor supply-chain events and patterns as they happen,"[71] but this limited version has drawbacks. "A business continuity-planning dashboard [can be used] to mitigate risks [by helping] to respond to the disaster as it [occurs],"[72] and not to proactively reduce the risk. While not sufficient on their own to reduce risk, dashboards and risk mapping allow the company to build an understanding of the inputs and outputs of the system. This understanding ensures that connections between systems are understood, even before any

---

[67] In the U.S. military context, a military standard, MIL-STD-882E, contains a "Preliminary Hazard List" (Task 201) that performs a similar role.

[68] Supply Chain Risk Leadership Council, "Supply Chain Risk Management: A Compilation of Best Practices," August 2011.

[69] "Supply Chain Risk Leadership Council Supply Chain Risk Management Maturity Model," 2013b.

[70] Marchese and O'Dwyer, 2014.

[71] Deloitte Development LLC, *Supply Chain Resilience: A Risk Intelligent Approach to Managing Global Supply Chains*, part of the *Risk Intelligence Series*, 2013.

[72] Sáenz and Revilla, 2014.

changes are considered. In a real-time response situation, it is then possible to respond even when plans for the specific situation encountered do not exist.

Proactive risk management requires this deeper understanding of the system, not only to see the risks that are occurring and respond, but also to make changes to anticipate and reduce these risks. "Firms may choose to rank risk events based on a qualitative overall risk level [as] a simplistic approach . . . for the initial risk register,"[73] but most move on to more complex models to understand the relationships. This understanding then creates an additional use for creating a database of risks and potential strategies. Following this, simulations using the models or war gaming are used to understand impacts of risks and the benefits of the strategies considered. These "make it easier for companies to [understand] the overwhelming complexity of . . . risks [and decide on changes in order] to build resilience."[74] This process enables a company with a complete view of their systems to manage any risks that they have considered and that they are able to model.

Developing Resilience for Foreseen and Unforeseen Risks

As noted earlier, the types of risks encountered in understanding supply chains span an enormous range; anything that disrupts a supplier's business, operations, functions, or even the macroeconomic conditions can impact the supply chain. Foreseen risks can be managed using tools mentioned above, but with an evolving and changing supply chain, many caution that "contingency rules and procedures,"[75] "efforts to identify and mitigate,"[76] or even "ability to manage risks"[77] are insufficient. Instead, a more complete systemic resilience is called for. This is referred to in different contexts as "proactively [mitigating] risk,"[78] "balancing proactive mitigation capabilities with reactive capabilities,"[79] being "risk intelligent,"[80] or simply as resilience.[81]

Despite the importance of these methods, "tactical approaches to strengthening supply chain resilience are anything but clear. A spectrum of reasons drive this, including a lack of collaboration across functions, the cost of implementing resilient approaches, lacking the data needed, and an inability to measure the benefits of the strategies."[82] This means that the

---

[73] Supply Chain Risk Leadership Council, 2011.

[74] Deloitte Development LLC, 2013.

[75] Sáenz and Revilla, 2014.

[76] Deloitte Development LLC, 2013.

[77] Sheffi, 2005.

[78] Marchese and O'Dwyer, 2014.

[79] Sáenz and Revilla, 2014.

[80] Deloitte Development LLC, 2013.

[81] Sheffi, 2005.

[82] Marchese and O'Dwyer, 2014.

straightforward approaches mentioned above of modeling everything and picking options to minimize risk, or maximize profit under uncertainty, is not always feasible—even if a complete risk register could be developed. Instead, systemic (as opposed to tactical) approaches are worth considering. Even if the cost-benefit cannot be rigorously measured, many of these approaches are lower cost and have benefits that extend to a range of possible disruptions, even beyond those considered.

Taking Resilience Further

The view of resilience as a generalization of risk management allows for approaches driven by understanding the nature of the systems, as opposed to those driven by complex modeling or war gaming. The visibility that is achieved in order to respond to real-time risks can be leveraged to consider how the system itself can be changed to be less vulnerable. Beyond that, by considering how these more global methods to increase resilience can be used to address known threats, benefits that accrue will frequently also address unknown threats.

Yossi Sheffi, a pioneer in supply chain resilience, first addressed this issue, focusing on the concept of general resilience.[83] He lists three main ways to increase this general type of resilience: redundancy, flexibility, and cultural change. The first has limited utility, since it is the most expensive and most temporary option (a feature of supply chains, not necessarily other systems), while the second and third include many strategies that are both effective across domains and reasonable to implement.[84]

Flexibility is understood as the ability to withstand disruptions and respond accordingly. Three useful actions for attaining this flexibility are presented and include standardized processes, disaggregation, and postponing decisions and operations.[85] Standardized processes allow for easier reallocation of resources, interchangeable parts, and easier cross-training of personnel. Disaggregation—as it is referred to in this context ("concurrent instead of sequential processes")—allows for less disruption when a disrupting event occurs and speeds up recovery. Lastly, postponing decisions and operations until the last stages of the process both empowers those in charge and allows for more flexible operations when disruption occurs. This concept is closely related to distributed power, described in more detail below.

Cultural change is the last category listed by Sheffi, and while in some contexts, it is more difficult than others, the four ways to change it are useful to consider. The four ways are continuous communication, distributed decisionmaking power, passion for work, and training for disruption. Continuous communication allows employees that are affected by a disruption, or

---

[83] Sheffi, 2005.

[84] Sheffi, 2005.

[85] The fourth, "align procurement strategy with supplier relationships," is very specific to tightly integrated supply chains, and is useful in the specific context of collaborative or supply relationships, but might not apply more generally.

those in charge of the system disrupted, to understand the context of the problem, so that solutions can be found even when the system itself is disrupted. Distributed decisionmaking power allows employees to respond quickly, potentially limiting the impact or duration of a disruption. Passion for work makes employees willing to take steps beyond the basics in order to respond. Lastly, training for disruptions means that the company understands and routinely works around minor operational interruptions, and this allows major disruptions to be treated similarly.[86]

Case Study: Toyota's Supply-Chain Reassessment

Once an exemplar of supply-chain management, Toyota was well known in the business world of the 1940s and 1950s for developing innovative and efficient methods for supply-chain operations. Their supply chain was optimized, and their suppliers made parts quickly in response to demand, each source providing the components needed for the specific task or production process. Toyota had worked diligently over many years to remove slack from its supply operations by using just-in-time parts delivery to keep inventories to a minimum." In some cases, parts were only available from a single supplier.[87]

Cracks in the edifice emerged after the 2010 recall of more than seven million cars. This recall has been blamed in large part on "inadequate supplier management," by Jim Lawton of Dun & Bradstreet, an expert on supply-management solutions.[88] The company began to reevaluate their model of supply-chain management.[89]

The year after, in 2011, the Tōhoku earthquake and tsunami severely impacted Toyota's business. The head of purchasing noted that the "assumption that [Toyota] had a total grip on our supply chain proved to be an illusion."[90] Instead, they saw a decrease in global production of 30 percent due to what most would consider a foreseeable risk, an earthquake in an earthquake-prone region, and it took six months for the supply chain to recover.[91] As a result, in March 2012, Toyota announced a plan to reduce the time to recover to two weeks. The company unveiled a *Toyota New Global Architecture* plan that would be implemented fully by 2015,[92] but immediate work was also begun.

---

[86] Sheffi, 2005.

[87] Kelly Marchese and Bill Lam, "Toyota Pioneers New Global Supply Chains," *CIO Journal* (part of *Deloitte Insights*), August 12, 2014.

[88] Robert J. Bowman, "Blaming Toyota"s Supply Chain," *SupplyChainBrain.com*, 2010.

[89] SupplierBusiness.com, "Analysis: Supply Chain Management and the Crisis at Toyota," February 2, 2010.

[90] SCDigest Editorial Staff, "Global Supply Chain News: Toyota Taking Massive Effort to Reduce Its Supply Chain Risk in Japan," SCIDigest's *On-Target e-Magazine*, March 7, 2012.

[91] Marchese and Lam, 2014.

[92] IHS, "Toyota Announces Details of New Global Production Framework," March 29, 2013.

The first part of this work was the initial identification and implementation of plans for addressing risks. Toyota "used analytics and visualization tools to map [their] supply chain."[93] This was intended to allow for clearer understanding of the relationship between their providers and their processes. As noted earlier, visibility is a critical first step in being able to build response capacity. In some cases, they found, distinct suppliers relied on the same second-tier suppliers, making what looked like a disaggregated supply chain a fragile one instead.[94]

Next, Toyota began efforts to reduce the complexity of the process where possible, using standardization to increase flexibility. For example, they reduced the number of custom parts for their automobiles, moving from 50 types of airbags to only ten, and from 100 models of radiators to 21. The new standardized parts and processes "should make the company less vulnerable to supply disruptions by using parts from the largest manufacturers that can be substituted globally."[95] The visibility allowed them to address known risks by increasing standardization and flexibility.

The full measure of the change that Toyota is implementing will not be obvious until the next crisis, as the changes are intended to address their resilience to possible future events. We can see the critical types of issues that tightly integrated supply-chain systems without proper risk management can cause, and Toyota is attempting to build solutions using the best practices discussed. As is typical, the benefits of risk management are often seen in what does *not* happen, not what does. Cultural changes leading to new ways of thinking about risk, and the ability to prevent problems before they become crises, are exactly the goal of this type of work.

Summary: Adaptability and Supply-Chain Management

Mission success for business operations is enhanced by an ability to operate through a threat environment. Business operations seek to ensure long-term mission success, i.e., maximizing profits over some defined time span, by finding an optimal balance between efficiency of operations and minimizing vulnerability to disruption. Resilience is therefore achieved by balancing these competing objectives; lowered efficiency and increased resilience must be balanced against the reduced cost in cases of actual interruption. To assess resilience, businesses will often list risks and impacts and compare relative vulnerabilities to each. While this list cannot be exhaustive, strategies for resilience against known threats are pursued. Ideally the mitigations strategies, while specific to one type of threat, also harden the system against other threat types, both foreseen and unforeseen.

---

[93] Marchese and O'Dwyer, 2014.

[94] Marchese and O'Dwyer, 2014.

[95] Ma Jie and Masatsugu Horie, "Toyota Airbag Cuts Create Opening for Overseas Suppliers," *Bloomberg News* online, June 10, 2013.

The strategies for achieving resilience have two stages; the first involves increased information availability, while the second redesigns processes for flexibility. Not only does increased visibility expedite the detection of potential disruptions and enables impact mitigation from these disruptions as they occur, but the consequent increased situational awareness facilitates the identification of inefficiencies in the process. This increased information availability helps to mitigate impact even in the absence of a specific response plan, since all involved parties have the requisite knowledge to make informed operational decisions.

The second stage is to develop a proactive risk-management strategy by using the new understanding of all inputs and outputs affecting their operations. By redesigning processes with flexibility in mind, it is possible to reduce common points of vulnerability, increase flexibility, and build a dynamic culture that is able to respond more effectively. The methods used to reduce vulnerability and increase flexibility include redundancy, standardized processes and components, and disaggregating integrated operations. The methods used to build a dynamic culture include fostering continuous communication, distributing decisionmaking power, creating passion for work, and training for disruption.

The flexibility afforded through information flow, shared mission awareness, and processes that were redesigned with flexibility and adaptability in mind is key to mission resilience for a dynamic environment characterized by moderate risk, and increased information availability is the critical component for overall mission assurance.

5. Recover: Disaster Response and Recovery-Oriented Resilience

Disaster Response Procedures and Processes

In contrast to HROs that are designed to be failure resistant and business supply chains that are designed to operate through threat scenarios, some communities with high-priority missions instead are optimized for rapid recovery immediately following impact rather than avoiding or accommodating this impact. The reasons for this may include the degree of difficulty and expense required for hardening the organization to all possible threats, the large number of possible impacts that would need to be anticipated in order to avoid impact, and the sheer number of facilities that would need to be hardened to secure the entire system. This section addresses organizations that have perhaps a low tolerance for risk, but cannot feasibly harden themselves against this risk. While, in some circumstances, they may be able to operate through a disruption, they must also be prepared for significant degradation of capabilities in an emergency, and as such must be able effectively recover.

In the wake of a threat event of high impact, such as a natural disaster, some high-priority communities strive for rapid recovery of mission-critical capabilities even as they follow procedures to minimize impact. These types of organizations emphasize the ability to recover as a basic resilience metric, and organizations such as these include hospitals and utility companies. For instance, the recovery of basic capabilities in a hospital during and following a natural disaster will save lives, and the restoration of electricity following a power outage will not only facilitate ongoing recovery efforts, but could also prevent a larger system collapse and the severe economic impacts of such a blackout.[96] While all possible efforts are made to prevent and mitigate impact, optimizing recovery efforts is central to improving resilience for critical missions in this type of organization.

Preparing for Disaster Recovery

The Federal Emergency Management Agency (FEMA), an organization dedicated to disaster response, produces a National Disaster Recovery Framework (NDRF) that outlines several steps that an organization can take to support recovery efforts. The framework presented here is informed by past experience and asserts that the following are key attributes of successful recovery efforts: clear interagency cooperation, detailed planning, and clear but flexible

---

[96] Andrey Bernstein, Daniel Bienstock, David Hay, Meric Uzunoglu, Gil Zussman, "Power Grid Vulnerability to Geographically Correlated Failures—Analysis and Control Implications," *IEEE INFOCOM 2014 Proceedings*, 2014, pp. 2634–2642; Electric Consumer Resource Council (ELCON), "The Economic Impacts of the August 2003 Blackout," February 9, 2004.

decisionmaking hierarchies.[97] The effectiveness of disaster recovery is enhanced by clearly defining roles for the involved parties and their communication and collaboration structure. Further, "core recovery principles" that guide all action during this effort should be established and well understood by all involved parties. Establishing clear reporting structures and procedures and ensuring shared awareness of recovery goals mirror practices observed by HROs, discussed above. Communication is also stressed as a key component of a successful recovery, and interoperability of communication systems may support rapid recovery of services.[98] Overall, a plan for communication, collaboration, and resource allocation during the recovery efforts is vital and requires thoughtful preparation prior to any threat impact. These characteristics are emphasized in the NDRF, but implementation is exercised in practice with varying degrees of success. The following examples demonstrate elements of successful recovery and where the principles outlined in the NDRF surface and where they may fail.

An important aspect of preparing for disaster recovery is compiling and benefiting from lessons learned from past disasters. Similar again to the emphasis in HROs on learning from failures and near misses, important elements of resilience in disaster recovery include identifying previous errors and correcting or improving processes. It is for this purpose that after-action reports are produced; these reports are published by institutions such as FEMA and the Department of Homeland Security to describe successful components of the response effort as well as identify challenges and room for improvement.[99] Previous hurricane-disaster response efforts can enhance subsequent hurricane-response plans due these after-action reports, as is demonstrated in this case study.

Responding to Disaster

The previous steps outline important measures to take in preparation prior to impact. An additional and vital step toward recovery takes place immediately following a threat impact: the identification and accurate assessment of the problem. Time to detect added to time to recovery is the primary metric used for this mission type or organization.[100] Network survivability models have been developed to identify vulnerable locations, and this information can be used to allocate monitoring resources at these vulnerable areas.[101] Another way to decrease response

---

[97] Federal Emergency Management Agency, National Disaster Recovery Framework: Strengthening Disaster Recovery for the Nation, September 2011.

[98] James L. Garnett and Alexander Kouzmin, "Communicating Throughout Katrina: Competing and Complementary Conceptual Lenses on Crisis Communication," Public Administration Review, Vol. 67, supplement 1, December 2007, pp. 171–188.

[99] For example, see report issued by FEMA, 2013.

[100] Jung-Chieh Chen, Wen-Tai Li, Chao-Kai Wen, Jen-Hao Teng, and Pangan Ting, "Efficient Identification Methods for Power Line Outages in the Smart Power Grid," IEEE Transactions on Power Systems, Vol. 29, No. 4, July 2014, pp. 1788–1800.

[101] Bernstein et al., 2014.

time is by automating the identification of failed nodes in the network. AT&T, for example, developed a linear programming model for optimizing restoration efforts following a network outage.[102] Using power grid operations as an example, during a power outage, the grid operator's first priority is to identify the source of the outage to avoid a grid-wide blackout. This can often be a nontrivial task in the face of multiple failures in the network, and the ability to quickly locate and assess the problem is a key component of grid resilience via rapid recovery.[103] Following detection, these failure sites must be prioritized for most efficient allocation of resources, and grid operators must develop procedures for making resource-allocation decisions.

Case Studies: Post-Hurricane Recovery Operations in the North Shore– Long Island Jewish Health System and Mississippi Power

Hospitals and utility companies both provide explicit examples of a community that has very low risk tolerance but for whom hardening all facilities to completely avoid impact is intractable. Hospital operations have an especially high vulnerability to disruptions due to their high level of complexity and inherently dynamic environment. The patients and their care requirements are constantly evolving, and the equipment used is often specialized and difficult to replace. The response of a hospital to a direct hit by a natural disaster is further complicated by the time criticality of many of their operations. For some critical patients, even a brief disruption in operations could be life threatening. Regardless of the impact, hospitals cannot just wait for the disruption to run its course and then resume operations.

Similarly, a failure in the electricity supply or other network service could have an enormous impact that could be compounded by the need for electricity or network communications to conduct many recovery operations. The power grid and all of its components are, for example, exceedingly complex, and even a small failure could cascade into a catastrophic outage. The following examples of disaster response following hurricane impact demonstrate lessons in restoring capability during and immediately following a disruption of service and illustrate two approaches: (1) transitioning to alternate infrastructure or facilities and (2) repairing existing facilities.

Utilization of Alternate Facilities

One way to recover operations is through relocation to alternate facilities. This approach allows operations to continue, even with system failure, by utilizing duplicate systems and capabilities. In this way, the approach can also be viewed as avoidance if the evacuation and relocation takes place prior to the loss of capabilities. The evacuation procedures undertaken by the North Shore– Long Island Jewish Health System in response to Hurricane Irene in August 2011 demonstrate

---

[102] Chen et al., 2014

[103] Chen et al., 2014.

29

the importance of planning and the challenges associated with large-scale relocation under severe time constraints. This hospital is a network of hospitals serving about 7 million people in the New York metropolitan area; it is the largest integrated health care network in the state of New York. Three of the sixteen hospitals in this network are located in areas prone to flooding, and about one-thousand patients in these three hospitals were required to be evacuated in just under three days in anticipation of severe impact from Hurricane Irene.[104] Despite the size and complexity of the evacuation effort, this system of hospitals successfully evacuated 947 patients without any deaths or injuries from three separate facilities.[105]

This example demonstrates a successful implementation of the planning component stressed in the NDRF. Perhaps, even more importantly, is that the success of this relocation effort was made possible largely due to previous failures. The key to the success of this evacuation comes from lessons learned from previous experience with natural disasters. Following the challenges and failures observed during the emergency response to Hurricane Katrina, hospitals were able to revise their own response plans accordingly. After-action reports include an issuance from the Texas Department of State Health Services that outlines the failure to adequately track patients during Katrina, including the inability to transfer pertinent medical information with patients.[106] Recognizing the need for more efficient means of transferring patients, hospital administrators implemented a full-scale evacuation exercise that moved actual simulated patients.[107] A common approach for hospitals under evacuation is to work one at a time to identify appropriate facilities for each patient to be evacuated, and this is how this full-scale exercise was first conducted. This approach is often extremely cumbersome; processing each patient one by one is time consuming, and arranging transport on a patient-by-patient basis instead of optimizing according to location can make the operation extremely inefficient. During these exercises, hospital administrators became aware of this inefficiency and, in response, developed a new approach that instead categorized patients by the types of clinical services they needed and transported them to hospitals that could match these needs. This ability to not only exercise response plans but also to adjust to incorporate a more optimized approach was key to the success of the hospital evacuation during Hurricane Irene. This reinforces the importance of planning outlined in the NDRF, but expands this to emphasize not only the existence of a plan, but also the ability to practice this plan in a realistic setting and adjust accordingly based on the results of this exercise.

---

[104] Christina Verni, "A Hospital System's Reponse to a Hurricane Offers Lessons, Including the Need for Mandatory Interfacility Drills," *Health Affairs*, Vol. 31, No. 8, 2012, pp. 1841–1821.

[105] Verni, 2012.

[106] Litaker Group, LLC, "The Health and Medical Response to Hurricanes Katrina and Rita by the Texas Department of State Health Services: After Action Report," prepared for the Texas Department of State Health Surfaces, June 5, 2006

[107] Verni, 2012.

Successful Repair and Recover Operations

Another way to recover operations is through repairing current systems and infrastructure following impact rather than to relocate operations. Power utilities and telecommunications networks represent industries that strive to repair and recover from outages as quickly as possible. While these large and complex network services, including communications and power distribution infrastructure, usually have extensive programs in place to mitigate impact and avoid failure, planning for failure response is integral to continued operations as extended outages would have a significant impact on a large customer base. In contrast to the hospital evacuation efforts described above, these recovery efforts are aimed at restoring operational capacity by repairing the damaged infrastructure.

The recovery efforts from Mississippi Power following Hurricane Katrina in 2005 demonstrate the vital role of a clearly outlined response plan and shared mission awareness. The impact of this storm left 100 percent of Mississippi Power's customers without power. Central to the response and recovery efforts undertaken by Mississippi Power was a continuously updated and well-rehearsed response plan, a clear reporting structure, availability of appropriately skilled personnel, and shared mission awareness.[108] An important contributor to Mississippi Power's successful effort to recover power service was the availability of skilled workers to bolster skill availability during an emergency. Retired linemen and field operations managers were on call in the wake of Hurricane Katrina's impact and, additionally, linemen are shared between utilities during emergencies.[109] This increases the overall experience level of personnel during this recovery effort. Personnel at every level understood the gravity of the overall mission, and this shared situational awareness supported a focused recovery effort. An established reporting structure and well-rehearsed response plan allowed line managers to identify high-priority needs and integrate information efficiently[110].

In addition to shared mission awareness and appropriate response planning, optimization of resources during recovery requires the ability to prioritize scarce resources. AT&T has developed an approach to restoration that seeks to optimize the response during an outage based on the existence of *restoration capacity*, a concept that refers to the ability to reroute traffic in the event of a network failure by using excess capacity in the network. This concept is guided by two principles. First, the restoration capacity must grow in tandem with the service capacity of the telecommunications network to maintain reliability.[111] Second, the determination of restoration capacity must consider the costs represented by lost revenue. Restoration capacity is a significant fraction of the infrastructure costs associated with telecommunication networks, so

---

[108] Smith, 2013.

[109] Smith, 2013.

[110] Smith, 2013.

[111] Ken Ambs, Sebastian Cwilich, Mei Deng, David J. Houck, David F. Lynch, and Dicky Yan, "Optimizing Restoration Capacity in the AT&T Network," *Interfaces*, Vol. 30, No. 1, February 1, 2000, pp. 26–44.

this investment must be carefully calibrated to maximize both profit and reliability.[112] Because this capacity represents such a large expense, AT&T invested significant effort into developing a network-planning tool that can optimize this capacity by quickly identifying restoration routes during a failure and rerouting according to priority. The development of this tool was enabled by a clear understanding of the demands and priorities by response planners and a methodical approach toward determining appropriate allocation of repair resources.

Summary: Disaster Recovery

Case-study reports on disaster recovery and response emphasize the importance of a clear reporting structure, rapid detection, and dynamic planning and response procedures. These concepts can be divided into two separate approaches: relocation to alternate backup facilities or rebuilding and restoring current infrastructure or facilities. Discussion of each response approach illustrates lessons for enhancing resilience through disaster recovery.

For the first approach, evacuation procedures in the face of a threat event, full-scale exercises conducted prior to the threat impact can reveal more efficient methods and time-saving measures that can be incorporated into a periodically edited emergency response plan. Incorporating lessons learned from response-planning exercises can significantly increase the efficiency and efficacy of future response efforts. In addition, guidelines for making the decision to evacuate and when should be well established prior to a threat event.

For the second approach, repairing and restoring infrastructure, having experienced personnel on call is a vital contributor to a timely recovery, along with shared mission awareness among all personnel and established and coordinated reporting procedures. During disaster response, time is critical, and the speed with which the source of the failure can be identified and addressed is the primary metric for resilience. Experienced personnel can more rapidly identify sources of failure and respond, resulting in significant reductions in loss. Coordination similarly minimizes response time by avoiding duplication of efforts and mitigating confusion if the activities need to divert from the response plan.

In both approaches, a dynamic emergency response plan that incorporates new information and is well rehearsed is a vital component of a successful recovery effort. Such a response plan will minimize response time by allowing efficient allocation of resources and strategic prioritization of efforts. Organizations that strive to recover from a threat impact quickly need to prepare and continuously update such a plan.

---

[112] Ambs et al., 2000.

6. Summary of Themes and Methods for Building Resilience

Challenges to Optimizing Resilience

Several paradoxical challenges exist in assuring resilience of a mission, and careful consideration of mission needs, risks, and capabilities can be required to reach an optimal compromise. Developing resilience against a specific threat can often make an organization more rigid and potentially more vulnerable to other general threats for which it is unprepared. Similarly, designing for resilience against a large number of threats may mean that the system is not optimized for resilience against any single threat. An organization must decide how to balance these two types of resilience. Organizational operations can be optimized for day-to-day operations that emphasize efficiency and longevity by streamlining processes and outsourcing activities. Often, however, what is ideal for robust day-to-day operations is not ideal during a threat event. Outsourced activities can become unreliable, compromising security or viability of the mission. Organizational structure that functions efficiently in a non-threat environment may be inflexible and intolerant of losses of leaders and communication nodes. The long-term health of the organization must therefore be considered alongside the short-term capabilities for addressing threats. Establishing resilient mission operations requires a consideration of both long- and short-term mission goals and identifying an appropriate allocation of resources to guard against known and unknown threats; each mission may require a unique approach.

Withstand, Adapt, Recover: Lessons Learned by Mission Type

Depending on the characteristics of the mission and the operational environment, resilience is approached in a variety of ways. While the objective, maintaining mission capability, for each approach is the same, mission capability can be achieved by avoiding impact, mitigating impact in real time, or recovering quickly from impact. Many organizations approach resilience with a combination of these concepts, and the academic literature and case-study reports offer guidance for developing an approach to assessing and enhancing resilience for each mission type described here.

Hazardous Industries and Ensuring Robustness

HROs illustrate best practices and lessons learned that could be applied to any operations with a low risk tolerance and severe consequences for failure. Avoiding impact is the objective for missions that are intolerant to any degradation in capability, and for these missions, robustness is the primary metric. The following concepts support resilient operations in a complex, integrated, and high-risk environment:

- Prepare for the full spectrum of impact, not the most likely impact, within practical and financial constraints.
- Establish shared mission awareness by optimizing access to information, emphasizing overall mission objectives, and supporting error reporting and identification of potential problems.
- Develop a clear reporting structure and ensure that accountability is established along this structure.
- Build system-specific training programs led by experts.
- Establish a clear hierarchy for decisionmaking, but balance this with appropriate flexibility allotted to personnel.

Adaptability and Supply Chain Management

The objective for missions taking place in a dynamic environment and that require the ability to operate through is mitigating impact. Here, adaptability and flexibility should be measured and evaluated as the primary metric for resilience. For business continuity planning, distributed power and standardized processing help to maximize flexibility when operating through a threat, while a dynamic culture allows the flexibility to be used effectively. Concepts that support continued mission capability include the following:

- Build a systematic approach to addressing threats, using methods that address specific threats in a way that will increase general resilience.
- Increase visibility to enhance efficiency and mitigate vulnerability.
- Support a comprehensive understanding of all operations to enable changes that increase flexibility and build a dynamic culture.
- Ensure flexibility of personnel and operations through standardized processes, disaggregation, and decision postponement.
- Build a dynamic culture by fostering continuous communication, distributing decisionmaking power, creating passion for work, and training for disruption.

Disaster Recovery Operations

Impact recovery is the objective for missions that cannot feasibly avoid impact, and the time and capacity to recover are the most appropriate resilience indicators. During disaster recovery, retaining experienced personnel on call that can quickly respond is highly effective for minimizing recovery time. The following concepts summarize methods for building resilience through rapid repair and recovery:

- Develop full-scale relocation exercises if backup facilities are part of the response plan.
- Establish a feedback loop for redesign of disaster-response plans that incorporates results from exercises.
- Ensure availability of experienced personnel.
- Establish a clear reporting structure to avoid duplication of efforts and to ensure efficient resource allocation during response.
- Develop a shared mission awareness and ensure collective efforts support a singular goal.

Common Themes for Increasing Resilience

While each of these mission types has unique resilience demands, they share several features and challenges. Common themes emerged throughout the literature and case-study reports, and these common themes offer guidance for increasing resilience regardless of mission type and threat environment. The following key components of resilient organizations reflect these common themes:

- Information sharing and shared awareness of mission.
- Clear reporting structures and cultures that support error reporting.
- Appropriate balance between flexible personnel with distributed decisionmaking and specialized personnel with centralized decisionmaking.
- Development of more accurate risk-assessment methods.
- Training for specific threats while maintaining flexibility in response procedures.

Information sharing and shared awareness of mission will increase the efficiency and effectiveness of operations both during and following a threat event. Implementing organizational structures and building internal cultures that support and encourage information flow and situation awareness are shown in the literature and case-study reports to optimize operations and personnel performance during and following a threat event or disruption. The Air Force could enhance resilience in the space community by finding ways to more effectively share information among personnel in different roles and at different levels of authority. This information sharing must be balanced, however, with effectiveness of operations and appropriate designation of decisionmaking authority. Overwhelming personnel with unneeded information could inhibit effective operations, thereby decreasing resilience; allowing personnel to make decisions based on partial information will also negatively impact operations. Organizations must therefore carefully evaluate how they can make as much information as possible available to decisionmakers without overwhelming them with extraneous data.

Clear reporting structures and cultures that support error reporting will allow an organization to develop more resilient operations by incorporating lessons from previous errors. Information flow is supported by a clear reporting structure that not only supports integrated communication, but also builds accountability. Establishing well-defined reporting procedures is shown to maximize the efficiency and timeliness of operations in each mission type discussed here, and developing a culture that supports the reporting of failures and near misses is a key element of this reporting structure. Similarly, the Air Force space community could build resilience by implementing measures to encourage error reporting free of the threat of reprimand and establishing ways to incorporate lessons from these errors in real time.

Appropriate balance between flexible personnel with distributed decisionmaking and specialized personnel with centralized decisionmaking. The ability to act outside of established response plans is key to building general resilience against unanticipated threats and impacts. Qualified personnel will have the ability to adapt responses in real time, and this ability needs to be accompanied by appropriate decisionmaking authority. Disaggregation of this authority during a threat response will enable swift response and action. Training programs in the Air Force could be adapted to ensure personnel have the expertise required to react in real time. However, distributed decisionmaking is more challenging for a large organization, and the Air Force may find that incorporating a more distributed authority may compromise the efficiency of its day-to-day operations. For this reason, a balance needs to be achieved between the flexibility of the personnel and their level of specialization; an inflexible hierarchy is brittle, but full authority being granted to all personnel is also brittle. The location of this balance is often challenging to identify and is determined by a variety of factors, including organizational size, operational requirements, and personnel skill level. Maximizing expertise and flexibility within this balance will support the ability to observe and react appropriately, in the manner of organizations that demonstrate collective mindfulness.

Accurate risk-assessment methods will facilitate better design and planning. While the full spectrum of possible impacts and risks may be impossible to capture, an accurate assessment of risk and failure tolerance will facilitate resource allocation and investment decisions. The Air Force could enhance their resilience by investing resources in risk-assessment modeling and fault-tolerance testing not just of individual critical elements but also of the system as a whole. In addition, consideration of mission and operation type can inform fault-tolerance requirements. For example, systems used for risk-averse missions should be designed to withstand maximum failure, while systems used to operate through a threat should be designed for maximum flexibility.

Training for specific threats while maintaining flexibility in response procedures is a challenge, but meeting this challenge will allow an organization to address both specific and general threats. Developing appropriate training programs is a vital step toward ensuring effective response to a threat event, and detailed exercises that address specific and known threats are crucial. However, unanticipated threats require personnel flexibility to respond outside of programmed procedures, and this presents a paradoxical challenge to operational managers, requiring compromise between efficient day-to-day operations and maximizing flexibility for disaster response. Increasing the frequency of detailed exercises would result in the Air Force being more prepared for these specific threat events, but ensuring that ad hoc response capabilities are developed needs to be similarly prioritized.

Conclusion

Each of the lessons identified in this report represents general assessments from the academic literature and reported experiences from case-study documentation. The value in presenting these concepts and hypotheses here is to enable organizations such as the Air Force to identify those measures that are most feasible based on mission requirements and cost. The general recommendations presented here, when placed in the context of a specific mission or goal, could provide specific steps for addressing resilience. For example, measures that require moderate effort for implementation may include the development of a feedback loop for building more dynamic emergency procedures or increasing the ability to integrate information. More challenging steps may include the development of large-scale exercises for assessing possible risks and improvements. Resource availability and an assessment of the impact of these measures will guide decisions on how to best approach resilience enhancement for each organization. Further analysis on assessing resilience for Air Force space operations can be found in the main report for this project as well as the report on the accompanying model.[113]

In general the intent of this overview was to provide a general framework for identifying appropriate measures for enhancing mission resilience, with each approach distinguished based on risk tolerance, mission needs, and threat environment. While this report has provided a general framework for identifying appropriate measures for addressing resilience, many additional and alternative views exist beyond the scope of this report. However, the approaches outlined here reflect a substantial spectrum of literature on the topic and could serve as a guide to identifying effective measures for optimizing mission capability in all of these cases.

---

[113] McLeod et al., 2016, and Paul Dreyer, Krista S. Langeland, David Manheim, Gary McLeod, and George Nacouzi, *RAPAPORT (Resilience Assessment Process and Portfolio Option Reporting Tool): Background and Method*, RR-1169-AF, Santa Monica, Calif.: RAND Corporation, RR-1169-AF, 2016.

References

Acton, James M., and Mark Hibbs, "Why Fukushima Was Preventable," *Carnegie Endowment for International Peace,* March 6, 2012. As of October 28, 2015:
http://carnegieendowment.org/2012/03/06/why-fukushima-was-preventable

Air Force Space Command, "Resiliency and Disaggregated Space Architectures," white paper, Peterson AFB, Colo., undated (released August 21, 2013). As of December 9, 2015:
http://www.afspc.af.mil/shared/media/document/AFD-130821-034.pdf

Ambs, Ken, Sebastian Cwilich, Mei Deng, David J. Houck, David F. Lynch, and Dicky Yan, "Optimizing Restoration Capacity in the AT&T Network," *Interfaces*, Vol. 30, No. 1, February 1, 2000, pp. 26–44.

Baker, David P., Rachel Day, and Eduardo Salas, "Teamwork as an Essential Component of High Reliability Organizations," *Health Services Research*, Vol. 41, No. 4, Part II, August 2006, pp. 1576–1598.

Baral, Nabin, "What Makes Grassroots Conservation Organizations Resilient? An Empirical Analysis of Diversity, Organizational Memory, and the Number of Leaders," *Environmental Management*, Vol. 51, No. 3, March 2013, pp. 738–749.

Bernstein, Andrey, Daniel Bienstock, David Hay, Meric Uzunoglu, Gil Zussman, "Power Grid Vulnerability to Geographically Correlated Failures—Analysis and Control Implications," *IEEE INFOCOM 2014 Proceedings*, 2014, pp. 2634–2642.

Bonanno, George A., "Loss, Trauma, and Human Resilience: Have We Underestimated the Human Capacity to Thrive After Extremely Aversive Events?" *American Psychologist*, Vol. 59, No. January 2004, pp. 20–28.

Bowman, Robert J., "Blaming Toyota's Supply Chain," *SupplyChainBrain.com*, 2010. As of September 23, 2014:
http://www.supplychainbrain.com/content/blogs/think-tank/blog/article/font-size2blaming-toyotas-supply-chainfont

Buckley, Walter, "Society as a Complex Adaptive System," in Walter Buckley, ed., *Modern Systems Research for the Behavioral Scientist*, Chicago, Ill.: Aldine Publishing Company, 1968, pp. 490–513.

Carpenter, Steve, Brian Walker, J. Marty Anderies, and Nick Abel, "From Metaphor to Measurement: Resilience of What to What?" *Ecosystems*, Vol. 4, No. 8, December 2001, pp. 765–781.

Chen, Jung-Chieh, Wen-Tai Li, Chao-Kai Wen, Jen-Hao Teng, and Pangan Ting, "Efficient Identification Methods for Power Line Outages in the Smart Power Grid," *IEEE Transactions on Power Systems*, Vol. 29, No. 4, July 2014, pp. 1788–1800.

Cook, R., and J. Rasmussen, "Going Solid: A Model of System Dynamics and Consequences for Patient Safety," *Quality and Safety in Health Care*, Vol. 14, 2005, pp. 130–134.

Deloitte Development LLC, *Supply Chain Resilience: A Risk Intelligent Approach to Managing Global Supply Chains*, part of the *Risk Intelligence Series*, 2013. As of October 28, 2015: http://www2.deloitte.com/content/dam/Deloitte/global/Documents/Governance-Risk-Compliance/dttl-grc-supplychainresilience-riskintelligentapproachtomanagingglobalsupplychains.pdf

Dreyer, Paul, Krista S. Langeland, David Manheim, Gary McLeod, and George Nacouzi, *RAPAPORT (Resilience Assessment Process and Portfolio Option Reporting Tool): Background and Method*, Santa Monica, Calif.: RAND Corporation, RR-1169-AF, 2016. As of April 2016: http://www.rand.org/pubs/research_reports/RR1169.html

Electric Consumer Resource Council (ELCON), "The Economic Impacts of the August 2003 Blackout," February 9, 2004. As of October 28, 2015: http://www.elcon.org/Documents/Profiles%20and%20Publications/Economic%20Impacts%20of%20August%202003%20Blackout.pdf

Emergency Management Assistance Compact, *Emergency Management Assistance Compact (EMAC) 2005 Hurricane Season Response After-Action Report*, undated. As of January 18, 2016: http://podcast.tisp.org/index.cfm?pk=download&id=10978&pid=10261

Federal Emergency Management Agency, *National Disaster Recovery Framework: Strengthening Disaster Recovery for the Nation*, September 2011. As of October 30, 2015: http://www.fema.gov/pdf/recoveryframework/ndrf.pdf

Garnett, James L., and Alexander Kouzmin, "Communicating Throughout Katrina: Competing and Complementary Conceptual Lenses on Crisis Communication," *Public Administration Review*, Vol. 67, supplement 1, December 2007, pp. 171–188.

Hirano, Masashi, Taisuke Yonomoto, Masahiro Ishigaki, Norio Watanabe, Yu Maruyama, Yasuteru Sibamoto, Tadashi Watanabe, and Kiyofumi Moriyama, "Insights from Review and Analysis of the Fukushima Dai-Ichi Accident," *Journal of Nuclear Science and Technology*, Vol. 49, No. 1, January 2012, pp. 1–17.

IHS, "Toyota Announces Details of New Global Production Framework," March 29, 2013. As of October 25, 2015: https://www.ihs.com/country-industry-forecasting.html?ID=1065977663

International Atomic Energy Agency, "Report of Japanese Government to the IAEA Ministerial Conference on Nuclear Safety—Accident at TEPCO's Fukushima Nuclear Power Stations," June 7, 2011a. As of October 30, 2015:
https://www.iaea.org/newscenter/focus/fukushima/japan-report

———, *The Operating Organization for Nuclear Power Plants, IAEA Safety Standards Series No. NS-G-2.4*, Vienna: International Atomic Energy Agency, 2011b. As of October 30, 2015:
http://www-pub.iaea.org/MTCD/Publications/PDF/Pub1115_scr.pdf

International Organization for Standardization (ISO), "Bases for Design of Structures—General Requirements," ISO 22111:2007, undated. As of October 28, 2015:
https://www.iso.org/obp/ui/#iso:std:iso:22111:ed-1:v1:en

Jennings, Barbara J., Eric D. Vugrin, and Deborah K. Belasich, "Resilience Certification for Commercial Buildings: A Study of Stakeholder Perspective," *Environment Systems and Decisions*, Vol. 33, 2013, pp. 184–194.

Jie, Ma, and Masatsugu Horie, "Toyota Airbag Cuts Create Opening for Overseas Suppliers," *Bloomberg News* online, June 10, 2013. As of September 23, 2014:
http://www.bloomberg.com/news/2013-06-09/toyota-airbag-cuts-create-opening-for-overseas-suppliers.html

Kohn, Linda T., Janet M. Corrigan, and Molla S. Donaldson, eds., *To Err is Human: Building a Safer Health System*, Washington, D.C.: National Academies Press, 2000.

LaPorte, Todd R., "High Reliability Organizations: Unlikely, Demanding, and At Risk," *Journal of Contingencies and Crisis Management*, Vol. 4, No. 2, June 1996, pp. 60–71.

Litaker Group, LLC, "The Health and Medical Response to Hurricanes Katrina and Rita by the Texas Department of State Health Services: After Action Report," prepared for the Texas Department of State Health Surfaces, June 5, 2006. As of February 16, 2015:
http://www.litakergroup.com/3_Litaker_Group_DSHS_AAR_June_2006.pdf

Marchese, Kelly, and Bill Lam, "Toyota Pioneers New Global Supply Chains," *CIO Journal* (part of *Deloitte Insights*), August 12, 2014. As of September 23, 2014:
http://deloitte.wsj.com/cio/2014/08/12/toyota-pioneers-new-global-supply-chains

Marchese, Kelly, and Jerry O'Dwyer, "From Risk to Resilience: Using Analytics and Visualization to Reduce Supply Chain Vulnerability," *Deloitte Review*, Issue 14, January 17, 2014. As of September 28, 2014:
http://dupress.com/articles/dr14-risk-to-resilience

McLeod, Gary, George Nacouzi, Paul Dryer, Mel Eisman, Myron Hura, Krista S. Langeland, David Manheim, and Geoffrey Torrington, *Enhancing Space Resilience Through Non-Materiel Means*, Santa Monica, Calif.: RAND Corporation, RR-1067-AF, 2016. As of April

2016:
http://www.rand.org/pubs/research_reports/RR1067.html

Meyer, Alan D., "Adapting to Environmental Jolts," *Administrative Science Quarterly*, Vol. 27, No. 4, December 1982, pp. 515–537.

Moingeon, Bertrand, and Amy Edmondson, eds., *Organizational Learning and Competitive Advantage*, London: Sage Publications, Ltd., 1996.

Park, J., T. P. Seager, P. S. C. Rao, M. Convertino, and I. Linkov, "Integrating Risk and Resilience Approaches to Catastrophe Management in Engineering Systems," *Risk Analysis*, Vol. 33, No. 3, 2013, pp. 356–367.

Perrow, Charles, *Normal Accidents: Living with High-Risk Technologies*, updated edition, Princeton, N.J.: Princeton University Press, 1999.

Psychology Today online, "Resilience: All About Resilience," undated. As of October 30, 2015: http://www.psychologytoday.com/basics/resilience

Roberts, Karlene H., "Some Characteristics of One Type of High Reliability Organization," *Organization Science*, Vol. 1, No. 2, 1990, pp. 160.

Sáenz, Maria Jesús, and Elena Revilla, "Creating More Resilient Supply Chains," *MIT Sloan Management Review*, Summer 2014. As of September 23, 2014: http://sloanreview.mit.edu/article/creating-more-resilient-supply-chains

SCDigest Editorial Staff, "Global Supply Chain News: Toyota Taking Massive Effort to Reduce Its Supply Chain Risk in Japan," SCIDigest's *On-Target e-Magazine*, March 7, 2012. As of September 23, 2015: http://www.scdigest.com/ontarget/12-03-07-2.php?cid=5576&ctype=content

Sheffi, Yossi, "Building a Resilient Supply Chain," *Harvard Business Review Supply Chain Strategy* newsletter, Vol. 1, No. 8, October 2005. As of September 23, 2014: http://sheffi.mit.edu/sites/default/files/genmedia.buildingresilientsupplychain.pdf

Smith, James Pat, and Gulfport CARRI Team, "Organizational Resilience: Mississippi Power as a Case Study," *A Gulfport Resilience Essay of the Community and Regional Resilience Institute,* March 2013. As of October 30, 2015: http://www.resilientus.org/wp-content/uploads/2013/03/GP_Resilience_Essay_Mississippi_Power_Case_Study_1249429862.pdf

Sugimori, Y., K. Kusunoki, F. Cho, and S. Uchikawa, "Toyota Production System and Kanban System: Materialization of Just-in-Time and Respect-for-Human System," *International Journal of Production Research*, Vol. 15, No. 6. 1977, pp. 553–564.

SupplierBusiness.com, "Analysis: Supply Chain Management and the Crisis at Toyota," February 2, 2010. As of September 23, 2014: http://www.just-auto.com/comment/supply-chain-management-and-the-crisis-at-toyota_id102995.aspx

Supply Chain Risk Leadership Council, "SCRLC Emerging Risks in the Supply Chain 2013," white paper, 2013. As of September 23, 2014: http://www.scrlc.com/articles/Emerging_Risks_2013_feb_v10.pdf

———, "Supply Chain Risk Management: A Compilation of Best Practices," August 2011. As of September 23, 2014: http://www.scrlc.com/articles/Supply_Chain_Risk_Management_A_Compilation_of_Best_Practices_final%5B1%5D.pdf

"Supply Chain Risk Leadership Council Supply Chain Risk Management Maturity Model," Microsoft Excel tool, April 2, 2013. As of September 23, 2014: http://www.supplychainriskinsights.com/pdf/scrlc_maturity_model_final_with_scoring_locked_2april2013.xlsx

Tokyo Electric Power Company, Inc. (TEPCO), "Fukushima Nuclear Accident Analysis Report," June 20, 2012. As of October 30, 2015: http://www.tepco.co.jp/en/press/corp-com/release/betu12_e/images/120620e0104.pdf

Tetlock, Philip E., "Accountability: A Social Check on the Fundamental Attribution Error," *Social Psychology Quarterly*, Vol. 48, No. 3, September 1985, pp. 227–236.

U.S. Department of Homeland Security, "National Preparedness Guidelines," updated August 15, 2015. As of October 28, 2015: http://www.dhs.gov/national-preparedness-guidelines

U.S. Nuclear Regulatory Commission, "Beyond Design-Basis Accidents," updated July 23, 2015. As of September 28, 2014: http://www.nrc.gov/reading-rm/basic-ref/glossary/beyond-design-basis-accidents.html

Verni, Christina, "A Hospital System's Reponse to a Hurricane Offers Lessons, Including the Need for Mandatory Interfacility Drills," *Health Affairs*, Vol. 31, No. 8, 2012, pp. 1841–1821.

Vogus, Timothy J., and Kathleen M. Sutcliffe, "Organizational Resilience: Towards a Theory and Research Agenda," *ISIC IEEE Conference on Systems, Man, and Cybernetics*, October 2007, pp. 3418–3422.

Weick, Karl E., "Organizational Culture as a Source of High Reliability," *California Management Review*, Vol. 29, No. 2, Winter 1987, pp. 112–127.

Weick, Karl E., Kathleen M. Sutcliffe, and David Obstfeld, "Organizing for High Reliability: Processes of Collective Mindfulness," in R.S. Sutton and B. M. Staw, eds., *Research in Organizational Behavior*, Vol. 1, Stanford, Calif.: Jai Press, 1999, pp. 81–123.

Weissman, Joel S., Catherine L. Annas, Arnold M. Epstein, Eric C. Schneider, Brian Clarridge, Leslie Kirle, Constantine Gatsonis, Sandra Feibelmann, and Nancy Ridley, "Error Reporting and Disclosure Systems: Views from Hospital Leaders," *Journal of the American Medical Association*, Vol. 293, No. 11, March 16, 2005, pp. 1359–1366.

———, *National Space Policy of the United States of America*, June 28, 2010. As of September 28, 2014:
http://www.whitehouse.gov/sites/default/files/national_space_policy_6-28-10.pdf

Wildavsky, Aaron B., *Searching for Safety*, Piscataway, N.J.: Transaction Publishers, 1988.

Wolf, Zane Robinson, and Ronda G. Hughes, "Error Reporting and Disclosure," in Ronda G. Hughes, ed., *Patient Safety and Quality: An Evidence-Based Handbook for Nurses*, Rockville, Md.: Agency for Healthcare Research and Quality, 2008, chapter 35.

Zolli, Andrew, and Ann Marie Healy, *Resilience: Why Things Bounce Back*, New York: Simon and Schuster, Inc., 2012, p. 7.